D1624690

PRAISE FOR
CAREER CHOREOGRAPHY™

"Ken Lindner's brilliant strategies have certainly helped shape and grow my career. Now, he shares his wonderful insights with you in his new book, *Career Choreography*."

—Mario Lopez, American host, actor, author, producer

"*Career Choreography* is exactly what people need right now! This book is magic! Ken Lindner has been choreographing my career at NBC News, MSNBC, and now CNN Headline News for over a decade with his one-of-a-kind-technique. At a time when so many crave a clear job and career direction, Ken's spot-on professional strategies and steps are invaluable for everyone who wants a fulfilling job and professional path. No one develops careers and crafts successful strategies like Ken Lindner."

—Lynn Smith, *Headline News* anchor and author

"Ken Lindner has devoted his career to helping people find, secure, and thrive in the jobs they covet. His *Career Choreography* strategies are a masterful roadmap to success."

—Philip D. M. de Picciotto, founder and president, Octagon Sports and Entertainment Network

"Every copy of *Career Choreography* should be wrapped with a big, green bow because—make *no* mistake—it is a gift to anyone working to achieve the kind of success most only dream of. Ken Lindner not only rewrites the old-school definition of success to include inner happiness and fulfillment, which have incredibly valuable currencies of their own, but then takes us to the yellow brick road and choreographs the journey for us. No matter what industry you hope to conquer, *Career Choreography* will give you the universal steps that will get you dancing to the top."

—**Liz Claman,** host of *The Claman Countdown* on the Fox Business Network and author

"Ken Lindner has an extraordinary talent and track record for creating successful careers for his clients. Trust the advice of the best career developer in the business! I speak from many wonderful years of positive experience with Ken. If you want to join or re-join the workforce in a fulfilling and rewarding position, that's suited to you and your special talents, *Career Choreography* is a must-read!"

—**Ernie Anastos,** Emmy Award–winning NYC television news icon and author

"'I am the master of my fate and captain of my soul' are the *Invictus* words of William Ernest Henley that provide hope for all of us in the journey of our lives and careers. Ken Lindner's new, masterful book, *Career Choreography*, is an outstanding tool that confers upon each of us the essential concepts and techniques that facilitate success in career and life. Over his illustrious career, Ken has been the agent to hundreds of the most successful TV news anchors and personalities. He is the agent of change, omnipresent teacher, mentor, and consultant that helps all of us develop our mission, vision, and concise and focused plans. *Career Choreography* is a must-read that depicts real-life examples and stories that illuminate tactics and strategies that we all can use in each of our playbooks."

—**Bert R. Mandelbaum, MD DHL (hon),** co-chair of medical affairs, Cedars-Sinai Kerlan-Jobe Institute and author of *The Win Within: Capturing Your Victorious Spirit*

"I've depended on Ken Lindner's advice and career consultation for a quarter of a century! Like shoe-leather reporting, his *Career Choreography* values hard work, discipline, and delayed gratification. But his emphasis on finding the right job fit was the secret sauce that pointed me in the direction of my dreams and a fulfilling career bringing you the morning news!"

—**Robin Meade,** anchor, *Morning Express with Robin Meade* on HLN

ALSO BY KEN LINDNER

*Your Killer Emotions: The 7 Steps to Mastering the
Toxic Emotions, Urges, and Impulses That Sabotage You*

*Crunch Time!: 8 Steps to Making the Right
Life Decisions at the Right Times*

*The New Broadcasting Realities:
Real-Life Strategies, Insights, and Issues for Broadcast
Journalists, Aspiring Journalists, Production Executives,
and Broadcasters in the New Age of Broadcasting,
Cable, and the Internet*

Your Step-by-Step Guide
to Finding the Right Job and Achieving
Huge Success and Happiness

CAREER
Choreography ™

Ken Lindner
America's Most Successful Career Developer

GREENLEAF
BOOK GROUP PRESS

Some of the stories, cases, and examples in this book are entirely fictional, and others have been fictionalized and altered to protect the privacy of the individuals involved (and their families). Such fictional or fictionalized stories, cases, and examples are not meant to portray any particular person, but instead are intended to poignantly and memorably illustrate the steps, strategies, and insights presented herein. To the extent that persons discussed in this book are either composites or entirely fictitious, references thereto are not meant to portray any particular real people, living or dead.

Published by Greenleaf Book Group Press
Austin, Texas
www.gbgpress.com

Copyright ©2021 Ken Lindner

All rights reserved.

Thank you for purchasing an authorized edition of this book and for complying with copyright law. No part of this book may be reproduced, stored in a retrieval system, or transmitted by any means, electronic, mechanical, photocopying, recording, or otherwise, without written permission from the copyright holder.

Distributed by Greenleaf Book Group

For ordering information or special discounts for bulk purchases, please contact Greenleaf Book Group at PO Box 91869, Austin, TX 78709, 512.891.6100.

Design and composition by Greenleaf Book Group
Cover design by Greenleaf Book Group

Publisher's Cataloging-in-Publication data is available.

Print ISBN: 978-1-62634-842-4

eBook ISBN: 978-1-62634-843-1

Part of the Tree Neutral® program, which offsets the number of trees consumed in the production and printing of this book by taking proactive steps, such as planting trees in direct proportion to the number of trees used: www.treeneutral.com

TreeNeutral

Printed in the United States of America on acid-free paper

21 22 23 24 25 26   10 9 8 7 6 5 4 3 2 1

First Edition

To my wonderful wife, Melinda, our two amazing children, Mary and Tristan, and our parents, Betty and Jack Lindner and Mary and Ross Myers.

CONTENTS

PART II: Career Choreography Strategies to Attain Huge Success Throughout Your Career Journey

PART III: Attaining True Career and Life Happiness

"The difference between trying and triumph
is an effective plan of action."

−KL

YOUR INTRODUCTION TO
CAREER CHOREOGRAPHY

I have the honor of owning what many believe is the finest and most well-respected television news and hosting agency in the world. Throughout the past thirty-five years, I have choreographed the careers of many thousands of this country's most successful and popular television newscasters and program hosts, as well as the careers of hugely successful entrepreneurs and professionals who now enjoy their most satisfying job.

The key to these individuals' extraordinary success is that they effectively practice the art of "Career Choreography." The term itself is one that I coined more than twenty-five years ago and then trade-marked. The first of the Four Principles of Career Choreography is its definition:

There is a logical, success-evoking choreography
for accomplishing all professional goals.
The key is to construct and implement the most
effective set of steps and strategies
in order to attain your goals.

Career Choreography enables you to craft your most rewarding career path, secure the job or position of your dreams, and be hugely successful at your position or profession.

Career Choreography will give you invaluable insights into the career strategies of such well-known individuals as Lester Holt, Mario Lopez, Megyn Kelly, Robin Meade, and Liz Claman. Within these pages, you will find instructive stories about many national and local anchors, hosts, and TV stars with whom I've worked. I have also included enlightening anecdotes about individuals with whom I haven't worked, such as Oprah Winfrey, LeBron James, and Katie Couric.

Additionally, there are insightful accounts about people who are not public figures, but whose stories will be highly beneficial and motivating for you. For instance, you will meet "Danielle,"[1] who left her tenuous real estate business during the 2008–2009 economic downturn to become a hugely successful salesperson of reality-based TV shows; "Heidi," who artfully crafted the steps to go from college graduation to, years later, living her dream of owning a fine art gallery; "Alan," who created a unique niche for his marriage-counseling practice that gave him the platform from which to write books, lecture, and exponentially increase his income; Jennifer, who began her career as a hair salon assistant and thereafter strategically worked to become the owner of two major hair salons and "the hair colorist to the stars"; Sam Weisbord, who went from the William Morris Agency mailroom to become the agency's president; "Sarah," a high-school senior who skillfully crafted a choreography that will enable her to become both a special-needs counselor and the stay-at-home mom she dearly aspires to be; and Jack Lindner, my dad, who didn't have a high-school education but persevered and went

---

1   Pseudonym.

on to enjoy two legendary executive careers that spanned more than eighty years. My dad's second career, during which he helped launch the T.J. Maxx department-store chain, began at age sixty-nine and lasted until he was ninety-eight. All of these individuals effectively utilized Career Choreography steps and strategies to attain their most treasured goals.

Personally, it has been through my being a lifelong "choreographer" that I have enjoyed enormously satisfying and rewarding life successes. I graduated from Harvard University, magna cum laude, and Cornell Law School. I was the captain and number-one singles and doubles player on the Harvard varsity tennis team and defeated Arthur Ashe in an exhibition match the year that Arthur was the fifth-ranked men's tennis player in the world. I am the CEO of Ken Lindner & Associates, Inc.; I am also the CEO of the International POP Tennis Association, Inc., as I am in large part responsible for choreographing the national and international growth of the sport of POP Tennis. I was inducted into the POP Tennis Hall of Fame as being one of the best players in its history. And, of course, I write and continually counsel individuals as to how to successfully choreograph their careers. When people ask how I accomplish all of these things and also spend so much time with my family, I tell them, "I'm an efficient choreographer."

I truly believe that *Career Choreography* will rock your world in tangible and wonderfully rewarding ways! Why am I so sure? Because these steps and strategies make sense, and they have brought huge success and career happiness to the thousands of individuals whom I've worked with over the past decades.

Career Choreography is divided into three parts. Part One is devoted to identifying and crafting the wisest and most beneficial career steps that will constitute your Career Choreographies. Part Two gives you the strategies to ensure that you will be extraordinarily successful and fulfilled in your chosen job, position, or profession. Part Three focuses on how to attain true career and life happiness.

WHY *CAREER CHOREOGRAPHY* IS ESSENTIAL FOR YOU

We are living in extremely challenging and debilitating times. Sadly, COVID-19 has killed an untold number of people, businesses, dreams, and plans. So many professional lives have been decimated, put on hold, or shrouded by uncertainty and the lack of a clear and effective game plan for moving forward. Individuals everywhere have had the emotional and psychological wind knocked out of them, and they don't have the tools or skill sets to rise from the canvas with confidence, fight on, and seize the job or career path they want.

The positive news is that the pandemic has given individuals worldwide the golden opportunity to reflect, assess, and tweak or reboot their professional plans and dreams. Just as there have been many jobs and businesses that have been lost or severely hurt due to the pandemic, there are new and exciting opportunities for creative, insightful, and forward-looking individuals to seize, as well as new niches to identify and voids to fill.

In the pandemic and post-pandemic new world, most professions, businesses, and commerce will function differently. New models and paradigms of doing business will be put into place. So it is an excellent time to be a superior adapter to our ever-changing normal, and to professionally thrive in our new world by being a highly astute and effective Career Choreographer.

I have dedicated my professional life to envisioning *what can be* in individuals and enabling them to attain their most prized goals by virtue of their efficacious creation and implementation of their individualized choreographies. At a time such as this, when so many cannot find their way or visualize their endgames, or don't have the knowledge, skill set, or discipline to implement and stick with their career game plans, the Four Principles of Career Choreography are an invaluable asset.

Career clarity and success-evoking choreographies are also essential for anyone mired in a no-growth or an unsatisfying job or career; for those entering the workforce for the first time, or reentering it; and for those who aspire to attain huge success in their current positions. Additionally, with all the mediocrity and self-sabotage that pervade the workplace, those armed with the most constructive strategies and mindsets can truly excel. Almost everyone needs and can materially benefit from a Career Choreography.

I firmly believe that *the difference between trying and triumph is an effective plan of action.* With this insight firmly in mind, let's begin choreographing your game-changing plan of action!

Part I

How to Identify and Craft Your Career Choreography

*Your goals are to make choices that reflect
your greatest aspirations, and thereafter act
consistently with those choices.*

—K.L.

YOUR KEY
CHOREOGRAPHY TERMS

As we start to lay a rock-solid, success-attaining foundation, let's define some of the key terms in this book, so that we are both working with the same understanding.

CHOREOGRAPHY

There is a logical and success-evoking choreography—or set of steps—for everything we want to accomplish. For example, you apply sunscreen and put on a hat *before* going into the sun, not afterward. You do this because it is the logical sequence of events in attaining your goal of reducing the risk of sunburn.

Throughout my counseling career, I have found that by visualizing, devising, and implementing a success-evoking game plan, my clients and I have consistently been able to attain our most cherished goals. If the choreography that you've developed is effective, it will maximize your time, your efforts, your skills, and your potential. All great things!

One of the keys to becoming the most adept choreographer possible, and to maximizing your results, is to understand and appreciate the interrelationship among (1) your values and/or desires, (2) your time, and (3) your capacity or ability to attain what you want.

In essence, each choreography aspires to be a set of well-thought-out and uniquely personal steps that will maximize (1) your time, (2) your capabilities/abilities, and ultimately (3) your results.

To illustrate, let's look at a real-life choreography that I needed to construct years ago.

Just before I boarded a plane from San Antonio, Texas, to Los Angeles, I called my parents and learned that my ninety-eight-year-old dad had become ill the night before. He had experienced trouble breathing and struggled to get out of bed and walk, which was uncharacteristic for him. This was of tremendous concern to both my mom and me.

Upon boarding the plane, I received a call from my office informing me of at least three client emergencies that needed to be dealt with as soon as I landed. At the conclusion of the call, my assistant, Shari, reminded me that I also had to rush from the L.A. airport to meet a landscaping crew at my home, so they could install a much-needed lighting system, as the system that I currently had wasn't working. This needed to be done as soon as possible, because after sunset, it would become pitch-black around my home and therefore dangerous for anyone who attempted to walk up to or around it.

To compound my time-crunch problem, a client was flying into L.A. for the evening to meet me for a seven-o'clock dinner. I also needed to return numerous personal and client phone calls and emails, pick up my dry cleaning, and gas up my car before going home to unpack and hit the hay.

Upon mentally listing all the things I needed to take care of upon my return to Los Angeles at 1:30 p.m., I asked myself my daily sanity-saving question:[2] "What is the most effective choreography

---

2   * No, *not* "Where's the Vicodin?"!

here (so I can accomplish everything that I need to in a timely and success-evoking manner)?"

In constructing my choreography, my first step was to list and prioritize my *values*. I needed to identify what was most important to me. In this instance, prioritization was easy. Of paramount importance was tending to my dad, followed by connecting with and counseling my clients through their emergencies, as well as keeping my dinner appointment with my client who was flying to L.A. for the evening. The fourth most pressing issue was to meet the landscapers at my home within an hour of my scheduled arrival in L.A. so that I could unlock the necessary doors and help direct them.

Next in importance was returning my other client calls—first to the ones on the East Coast and in the Midwest, and later, to those on the West Coast. After all those things were done, I could then get gas and pick up my dry cleaning, as the gas station and dry cleaner would be open late.

The pivotal question was: Did I have to see my dad immediately upon my arrival? Or could I see him a little later that afternoon? Before my plane took off for L.A., I called my mom, and she said my dad seemed to be feeling a bit better. We agreed that I would call her upon landing to see how he was doing. Basically, my dad's health status—my preeminent value—would dictate my choreography.

When I arrived in L.A., my mom told me that Dad was feeling much better. I spoke with him, and he did sound good. This allayed my concerns for the moment. I then called Shari and asked her to please push back my dinner date with my client from seven to eight, to change the location to a restaurant next to my office, and to email me the relevant client employment contracts and any other documents that I needed to read. By doing this, I would have the necessary materials in front of me when I counseled my clients after meeting with the landscapers.

I was then able to construct the choreography that maximized my time and my results. Here's how it played out.

1. I landed at LAX at 1:30 p.m., retrieved my luggage, and drove home.

2. While driving, I called the clients with emergencies to determine how best to counsel them.

3. I met with the landscapers at 2:30 and directed them.

4. While the landscapers installed the lighting system, I resumed counseling the clients with emergencies.

5. At 4:30, with the landscapers set up, I drove to my parents' home. During this trip, I resolved, as best as I could, my clients' emergencies. I then made East Coast client calls.

6. I spent time with my dad and mom between 5 and 6:30. Thankfully, my dad didn't seem to have any of the symptoms that had plagued him the night before.

7. I went across the street to my office and, from 6:45 until 7:45, I completed what seemed to be the most pressing West Coast calls. Shari told the remaining non-client callers that I would return their calls the following morning. (An effective choreography designer learns what tasks are wise to postpone for a later time.)

8. At 8, I met my client for dinner.

9. At 10:30, I filled my car and picked up my dry cleaning. A few moments later, I arrived home, and by 11:15, I was asleep.

This story shows that there is a logical order of acts that will maximize your chances of accomplishing your goals. As an effective choreographer, you will master the all-important art of valuing and ordering your priorities in a manner that enables you to attain your goals and dreams.

SUCCESS AND HAPPINESS

Merriam-Webster's Collegiate Dictionary defines "success" as "the attainment of wealth, favor, or eminence." Note that nowhere in this definition are the words "inner happiness," "harmony," or "fulfillment" found.

We will define "happy" as feeling or enjoying a state of contentment, fulfillment, satisfaction, or joy. Please keep in mind that what you deem to be success and happiness is a purely personal perspective, and the benchmark for either is entirely subjective.

CHOICES

The decisions we make are critically important, as they determine the course of our lives. They are like train tracks, in that trains go where the tracks take them. Similarly, our lives go where our choices take us. Our success and our happiness—or lack thereof—are a direct result of the choices we make. So these choices are precious. I have found that the difference between individuals who consistently fulfill their dreams and those who don't is that the former make constructive and self-enhancing choices on a consistent basis.

It is essential to recognize that when a choreography-impacting decision needs to be made, it should be consistent with your most highly prized goals and increase the percentages that you will achieve them.

One final thought for you on this: Never forget that, even during the most difficult times, you always have the luxury of being able to jump-start and lift your life by making constructive and self-enhancing choices.

POTENTIAL

"Potential" shall refer to the best of "what you can be" if you combine

a. your abilities;

b. your desire and passion;

c. a rock-solid intellectual and psychological skill set, where your emotions work in concert with your intellect to enable you to consistently make highly beneficial career choices; and

d. your ability to be an effective choreography designer and implementer.

One of my primary objectives is for you to come as close as possible to attaining your most positive potential.

CONSISTENT AND SUSTAINED
SUCCESS AND HAPPINESS

Another objective of *Career Choreography* is to equip you to achieve success and true happiness, time after time, throughout the rest of your life. This is why any reference to success and happiness will either explicitly or implicitly be preceded by the words "consistent" and "sustained." No one-hit wonders here!

CARPE DIEM

The spirit of *carpe diem*, Latin for "seize the day," lies at the heart of this material. For us, *carpe diem* is an acknowledgment of the fact that while you're alive, you always have opportunities to take steps that will put you in a position to fulfill your most positive potential and make your heart sing! Life's sweetest fruits are there for the taking. It's up to you as to whether you are committed to designing and taking the steps necessary to attain them.

The spirit of *carpe diem* implies that no matter where you are in your life—and no matter what you've gone through—starting today, you can still do positive, beneficial, and great things for your career and for your life! *Career Choreography* will show you how.

THE "8 CS OF SUCCESS"

Throughout *Career Choreography*, we will discuss in detail the "8 Cs of Success," which is your Career Choreography Principle 2. As you will learn, these words are packed with significance and meaning.

Choreograph your Career by Consistently implementing Conscious, Constructive, success-evoking Choices, made with Cognitive Clarity.

THE CONSCIOUS CHOICE

Before beneficial change can take place,
you must recognize that change is necessary
and be ready to implement that change.

—K.L.

W e have introduced the "8 Cs of Success," so let's begin by examining the "Conscious, Constructive Choice" compo-nent. Above all, being an effective Career Choreographer calls for you to consciously and consistently make constructive career choices and decisions. The word "conscious" for us means a clear, mindful intention to act in a specific manner, which is to honestly and non-defensively consider and weigh your values, and thereafter make a positive career decision. This process is an active one on your part, with you excited and hungry to raise the quality of your professional life by taking constructive action. The question you should pose to yourself is "Am I truly ready to make beneficial changes in my life?"

When answering this question, take your time and dig honestly and deeply into your heart of hearts. In developing individuals' careers for more than thirty-five years, I have found this exploration to be essential, because if you're not ready to identify your truest values, as well as acknowledge what's not working in your professional life, then in all likelihood you will not be nearly as successful as you will be when you are ready, engaged, and committed to the process.

Like snowflakes, we're all different, and we all have different developmental timetables. I was a late bloomer as a child—overweight, clumsy, and unfocused on schoolwork. Fortunately, my mom never compared my slow rate of development with that of other, more quickly maturing children. All I wanted to do as a youngster was play ball. It wasn't until I was a senior in high school that I found myself intellectually and emotionally ready and eager to embrace my schoolwork. With this new, committed mindset, I graduated magna cum laude from Harvard University. I enjoyed a similar experience with my athletic and professional endeavors. When I was psychologically and intellectually prepared to grow, I passionately made the most of both of these pursuits. So I understand how crucial it is to be authentically ready to embrace any new course of behavior.

An inspiring illustration of being ready to rise to the occasion involves former tennis professional James Blake. Prior to 2004, James had been moderately successful on the pro tour. Then, in 2004, three things happened that dramatically changed his life: His beloved father died of cancer, James crashed into the net post during a match and fractured vertebrae in his neck, and he contracted shingles, causing him vision problems in his left eye and temporary paralysis of his face.[3] His sudden health problems allegedly led James to believe that his tennis career was over.

Fortunately, James completely recovered from both physical

---

3   Chris Bowers, "Blake's Progress," *The Guardian*, June 23, 2007, https://www.theguardian .com/sport/2007/jun/24/tennis.wimbledon5.

setbacks. After a long and tedious road back, he convincingly won his first two matches of the 2005 U.S. Open. Just two days later, James shocked the tennis world by beating Rafael Nadal, the U.S. Open's second-seeded player, who had already won nine tournaments that year. In fact, James not only defeated Nadal but crushed him on one of the world's biggest tennis stages. James seemed to be playing better tennis *after* his illnesses and injuries than he ever had before.

How did this amazing feat at the U.S. Open take place? I believe that it was because James was in every way *ready* to take positive ownership of this part of his life!

So at this juncture, please take all the time you need to determine if you're committed to raising the quality, happiness, and satisfaction of your job or career. If you are, let's get started mastering the art of being a great Career Choreographer.

CHOREOGRAPHY REALITIES

As we move forward, it is crucial to remember that going through the process of designing and implementing a choreography entails just that—a process, not a quick fix. The progression is much more often akin to a marathon rather than a sprint. However, depending upon the difficulty of attaining the goal in question, the choreography at issue can involve just a few quick steps.

Also remember that choreography designers will often take gratifying steps forward as well as beneficial steps backward, and they must have the flexibility, creativity, and poise to be able to construct a new or modified step, or set of steps, when changes or unexpected events occur. Your goal is to be as adept as possible at being constructive and adaptable.

In implementing choreographies, you will experience plateaus as well as growth spurts. But even the most successful designers take some counterproductive or ineffective steps. They also may not effectively implement some of the right steps along the way. This is part and parcel of the exploration and growth processes. The key is for you to always keep your choreography and your *Big-Picture Goals* in mind while continuing to learn and grow from your victories, as well as from your missteps. If you are able to learn as you go, you thereby make all of your goal-attainment experiences constructive and self-enhancing. All of these learning experiences will be part of the rock-solid goal-attainment foundation that *Career Choreography* seeks to provide.

Before we move forward, please be aware of the two essential skills that all great choreographers possess: (1) the ability to construct a success-evoking set of steps that put you in a position to attain a specific goal or set of goals, and (2) the ability to effectively carry out—or implement—these steps. These are two distinctly different tasks, and they require different skill sets.

CHOREOGRAPHY CONSTRUCTION—WHAT DO YOU WANT TO ATTAIN?

*I urge you to answer the highest
calling of your heart . . .*

–JOHN LEWIS, civil rights leader

Whenever someone seeks my counsel regarding how to achieve any life or career goal, the first thought that comes to mind is "What is the most enhancing and sure-fire choreography we can construct, to put that person in a strong position to succeed and thereby raise their feelings of core confidence and self-esteem in the process?" The keys to being a great choreography designer are to—

1. *Visualize* "what can be" (what you want to attain).

2. *Identify* "what is" (where you are today).

3. *Contemplate* and *write down* the steps that will take you from where you are today to where you want to be, so that you can make your vision a reality.

Before you can construct the most effective goal-attainment steps, it is optimal to start your choreography by identifying *where* you want to end up or *what* you want to end up with.

Let's be clear here. Throughout every choreography, the successful construction and accomplishment of each step or strategy is a mini-goal attained. Your *Big-Picture Goal* or *"Goal"* is one of your primary goals. It is usually achieved through a series of choreography steps. Your *Gold-Ring Dream* or *"Dream"* is just that—it's what you want to accomplish above all else. Oftentimes, but not always, you must fulfill a series of *Goals* in order to live your *Dreams*. These *Goals* and *Dreams* are what every step that you've constructed and implemented is designed to culminate in. So, when constructing most choreographies, your first step is to identify—at the top of any page or *List*—your *Goal* or your *Dream*.

Essentially, this all-important choreography construction process focuses on valuation—you learning or confirming what you value most for yourself, your happiness and well-being, and your career. Your *Goals* and *Dreams* directly reflect your conscious and well-thought-out valuations. This brings us to Career Choreography Principle 3:

> Every career decision that you make and each career step that you take should reflect your most important life and career values, and bring you closer to attaining your career *Goals* and living your career *Dreams*.

Below are a few of the *Goals* and *Dreams* that some of my clients and I have identified:

1. "I want to own a public-relations company."

2. "I want to host *Good Morning America*."

3. "I want to have my own hair-color line."

4. "I want to be a partner in my firm."

5. "I want more meaning and job satisfaction from my work."

6. "I want to love what I do, be around interesting people, and have enough financial security to support my son and myself."

7. "I want to leave my career and my company and begin a whole new professional path. In essence, I'm ready for my second act."

8. "I want to get my first job in publishing."

9. "I want to incorporate my love of art, art galleries, and charity in whatever I do."

10. "I want to use my love of people, my entrepreneurial passion, my marketing skills, and my legal background in the job I take."

Throughout my counseling career, I've been surprised at the incredibly large number of people who don't take the necessary time or make the all-important effort to search deep down in their heart of hearts in order to ascertain what it is that they truly want to accomplish during their lifetime. As a result, most of these individuals are unfocused and directionless. It's no wonder so many people feel lost, empty, and unsatisfied! How can they feel fulfilled on a consistent basis if they haven't taken the focused time to learn who they are and what they really want? This insightful self-examination is an ongoing process, for with the passage of time, your values and *Goals* may change. Unquestionably, I have found that the individuals who achieve their *Goals* and fulfill their *Dreams* are the ones who

1. have a strong sense of what they want, or, at a minimum, know what they like to do and what they are good at;

2. can visualize *Goal* attainment ("If you can see it, you can far more easily *be* it");

3. have core confidence and believe their *Goal* is attainable ("You won't achieve it, if you don't believe it"); and

4. have a game plan or choreography as to how to attain their *Goal(s)*.

Through the years, I've identified some of the reasons why people don't take the requisite time to discern what they truly want. Often, it's because they perceive that they're simply too busy to do so, or that mining their true *Dreams* isn't worth the time. If you're one of these individuals, you probably waste tons of time flailing around, missing the mark, and being directionless, as opposed to maximizing your time and energy by taking logical, direct, success-evoking steps to attain your *Goals*.

As someone who wants to achieve your *Goals* and *Dreams*, starting today, you must make identifying your desires in life a major priority. I promise you that it will give you big-picture vision, clarity, direction, and focus—all qualities that *Goal* achievers have developed. Also remember that if you consistently flail, you'll probably fail!

By visualizing what you truly want, it will be much easier to be disciplined enough to stay on the often-difficult course of going for your *Dreams* and not opting for the immediate gratification of less-satisfying substitutes. Your *Goal* is to go for—and attain—life's gold, and not settle for the quick fix of less-gratifying brass.

In many instances, people don't search deep within to identify what they really want because they're afraid they might be faced with the stark reality of how far they've strayed from their heart's true *Dreams*, having settled and destructively compromised their *Goals*, their ideals, or themselves. Or they feel that the attainment of what they yearn for presents such a daunting or unattainable undertaking that they become timid and get depressed just thinking about it. This nonconstructive behavior is often caused by the way these individuals have been raised or by the consistent rejection or nonsuccess they have experienced in the past. As a result, these individuals are afraid to fail, or they are afraid to succeed, as they feel that one day they may be exposed as not really having the talent to warrant their success.

Later, we will deal with fear, and how it can severely retard your growth or paralyze you from taking constructive steps to better yourself. Since the beginning of my work as a Career Choreographer, I've empowered many clients to overcome their fears. For now, your *Goal* is to take the requisite steps to build your rock-solid, internal, *Goal*-attaining foundation by consciously crafting, taking, and mastering baby *Goal*-attainment step after baby *Goal*-attainment step. By carefully doing this, you develop your unshakable core confidence.

Before going on to the next section, I'd like you to identify what *you*—not your parents, not your spouse, not your friends, not your employer—truly want to attain in your professional life.

The key here is for you to commit the necessary time and energy to find a quiet place that allows you to decompress and break through the clutter of everything that is swirling around in your mind. I do this by taking long walks on the beach, bike rides, and scenic hikes. The prettier the scenery, the quieter the surroundings, and the fewer the distractions, the better. Find a place that transports you, moves you, inspires you, calms you, and/or makes you appreciative and introspective.

Once you're there, think about what would put a smile in your heart and on your face. Visualize a career *Goal* that energizes you and captures your imagination. Ask yourself: "What do I want to do with my career?" Dare to contemplate your truest and most exciting *Dreams*—no matter how far-fetched or distant they may appear.

Let your thoughts and imagination run wild, and allow your heart and soul to well up with the anticipation and visualization of what *can be*—as wonderful ideas and cherished *Dreams* come to mind. Feel like a kid again—when there seemed as if there were no boundaries or impediments.

This contemplation process, which we'll call the *Examination Process*, is essential. Keep in mind that even the most successful achievers have fallen short many times when endeavoring to fulfill their *Goals* and *Dreams*. So, as you go through the *Examination Process* and dig deep within, you may well feel pangs of sadness. This is part of the *Process*. It is commonplace to feel the deep pain of aspirations compromised or unfulfilled, and valuable time seemingly wasted. But be encouraged and assured that it's just as important to know what you *don't* want to do professionally as it is to know what you *do* want. For example, I worked for a corporate law firm during one of my law-school summers and disliked the experience. I learned that practicing law in that kind of an environment wasn't for me. This knowledge enabled me to move forward with a career that didn't include working for a law firm. Identifying what you don't want to do is just as much choreographer gold as discovering what makes your heart sing. Envision the great things you can and will attain, and what wonderful experiences and accomplishments you will enjoy by constructing the most effective choreographies.

Know that it is not at all unusual for the *Examination Process* to take many days, weeks, or months of quiet time in order to uncover what you cherish most. The following poem may inspire you. Be excited and have fun as you immerse yourself in the process of mining, exploring, and identifying what you *really* want in and from your job, profession, and career.

DISCERNING WHAT YOU REALLY WANT

If you want to know what lies deep inside,
You must drop your defenses and no longer hide,
And become the most effective sleuth,
By searching your heart and discerning the truth.

Don't pursue a goal 'cause you think it's expected,
As your emotional well-being can be negatively affected.
Don't try to attain goals, just because they're in fashion.
Make your heart sing! Follow your passion!

Seize a dream that will make you happy and proud,
Make the most of your life, don't play for the crowd.
'Cause in life there are few greater sins
Than ignoring the dreams you've repressed deep within.

—K.L.

YOUR *GOAL* AND *DREAM LISTS*

If you were able to identify the *Goals* or *Dreams* that you would like to attain, please write them down on your *Goal* and *Dream Lists*.[4]

---

4   You can find all of the *Lists* in this chapter in the appendix and download them at www.careerchoreography.com.

My *Big-Picture Goal(s)* is/are:

My *Dream(s)* is/are:

When constructing your *Goal-* or *Dream-*Attainment Choreography, your *Goal* or *Dream* will be at the top of your *List*. This *Goal* or *Dream* is the intended endpoint of all of the steps that you will construct.

A *Clarifying List* calls for you to write a list of all the things you love/like doing and those at which you excel. Your *Goal* is to home in on and clarify what positions and career paths you should consider or pursue. If you can't identify your *Goal* because you're still not sure what it is, then consider the following questions and write down your answers on your *Clarifying List*:

1. What makes you happy?

2. What do you like/love doing?

3. What are you good at?

4. What skills, experiences, and/or education do you have that would prepare you to have a fulfilling and successful career or experience in a particular field?

5. What do you not like doing or not want in your job or career?

Answering these questions may make it easier to identify your *Goals* or *Dreams*, and recognize *Goal-* and *Dream-*attaining opportunities when they are presented to you.

Let's study the case of "Heidi." Upon graduating with a journalism degree, she wasn't sure what she wanted to do with her professional life and found herself at a loss as to how to go about accomplishing her *Goals* once she identified them.

Since Heidi couldn't yet tell me what her *Goal* was, at my

suggestion, she took a good deal of time to go through her *Examination Process* and thereafter make a *Clarifying List* of her professional passions, including what she enjoys and what she is good at. Here, in essence, is her *Clarifying List*:

1. I love art, and I love studying it.

2. I love talking with artists and hearing about how they conceive and execute their visions.

3. I enjoy writing.

4. I enjoy interviewing people.

5. I enjoy public relations.

6. I enjoy helping others.

7. I enjoy doing charity work.

8. I love hosting both people and events.

9. I enjoy being creative and being a part of a creative community.

When Heidi completed her *Clarifying List*, I explained to her that many individuals—not just fresh college graduates—don't yet have a handle on what their *Goals* are, much less their *Dreams*. However, by identifying and clarifying what they like to do and what they're good at, they have a far better chance of constructing a Career Choreography that will bring them success, fulfillment, and happiness.

As Heidi and I continued our conversation, we both gleaned that being immersed in the art world was her true passion. Excellent! And, although writing was what she majored in, she wasn't nearly as passionate about it as she was about being in the art world; nor did having a career in writing seem like an attractive long-term *Goal*.

After further reflection on Heidi's part, she was certain that her *Dream* was to ultimately make her career in the art world; however, she agreed that some sort of writing position (her *Goal*) would work in the short term, as writing was her most marketable skill.

After some time and with great effort on Heidi's part, she secured a position writing about art at a well-respected magazine. A perfect start! Thirteen years later, after having myriad experiences and making some highly valuable contacts and friendships in the art world, Heidi fulfilled her *Dream* of co-owning—along with a financial backer—her own art gallery!

As a result, basically all of the criteria that Heidi had identified in her *Clarifying List*, years before, were satisfied. She now functions as the creative force behind her gallery, which she runs herself, and also has hosted a number of charity art auctions at her gallery. So, she even satisfied her desire to "host both people and events."

Heidi will be the first to tell you that she loves her work and her career because the work—which much of the time doesn't feel like work—makes her heart sing and is in harmony with who she is, what she is passionate about, and what she does well.

Heidi is a true Career Choreography success story.

Among the many things from Heidi's story that we can take away is the concept that in order to begin to construct the most success-evoking choreography, you must

1. identify your *Dream* or your *Goal*; or, if you don't know it,

2. identify, by constructing a *Clarifying List*, as Heidi did,

   a. the things you love/like to do,

b. the things you're good at doing, and

c. the areas in which you have acquired valuable experiences and education, both of which you would like to take advantage of.

Let's continue to explore the process of identifying *Goals* and *Dreams*.

Upon graduating from law school, I spent a great deal of time composing the following three *Clarifying Lists* that enabled me to identify what job would put me in the best position to be successful and derive great job enjoyment and satisfaction. My first *List*, entitled *What Will Make My Heart Sing and Cause Me to Look Forward to Going to Work Each Day?*, included the following:

a. First and foremost, working with people and being a nurturing and empowering "bright light" in their lives

b. Marketing a person, product, or idea that I believe in (I had done this when I began my group tennis-instruction business a few years earlier)

c. Being an integral part of the process of others fulfilling their *Dreams*

d. Being an entrepreneur and building a business, whether for myself or someone else

e. Practicing contract law

f. Visualizing "what can be" and choreographing steps to make it happen

g. Working with and learning from talented people

h. Being great at what I do

i. Working with and for individuals who inspire me, "get" me, believe in me, and believe that my success is their success

My second *List* was titled *What Are My Strengths, Skills, and Assets?* and read as follows:

a. I am trustworthy.

b. I am an effective and creative marketer.

c. I work well with people.

d. I am a creative, proactive thinker.

e. I have endless energy and enthusiasm in connection with endeavors that I enjoy and/or about which I'm passionate.

f. I'm a self-starter and self-deterministic.

g. I am much more comfortable leading than following.

h. Generally, people are motivated and inspired by my positive energy and outlook.

My final *List* was *What Do I NOT Like or Want to Do?* and included the following:

a. Be in a noncreative, fear-driven, conformist culture (what I learned about myself by working one summer for a corporate law firm)

b. Perform a job that primarily focuses upon projects, reports, and research and doesn't include a great deal of people-time

c. Be in an environment that doesn't allow me to be all that I can be and/or great at what I do

d. Be in a job that doesn't encourage me to be a creative and facile free spirit, entrepreneur, and marketer

e. Be in a job, profession, or career that I don't find fun, exciting, and challenging

f. Work for a company that doesn't appreciate me and my talents, contributions, and potential

g. Work for a company or with individuals whom I don't respect

Upon completing my three *Clarifying Lists*, it was much easier to decline opportunities that were inappropriate and seek out appropriate ones, as well as to identify and accept offers that put the percentages in my favor for me to be successful at and enjoy my work.

About a year after I composed my *Clarifying Lists*, I met with Sam Weisbord, the president of the William Morris Agency, which, at the time, was the most successful and well-respected talent agency in the country. Sam glowingly described agenting as the "people business" and listed a handful of the hundreds of world-renowned motion-picture, television, and music megastars that William Morris had represented through the years. When he detailed an agent's job description, I realized that not only would being a talent representative make my heart sing, but it also met almost all of the positive criteria that were in my *Clarifying Lists*. Being an agent called for—

1. Working with and guiding talented individuals in helping them achieve their *Goals* and *Dreams*

2. Marketing these individuals (the clients) to prospective employers, as well as marketing the William Morris Agency to these individuals if they were not yet clients of the agency

3. Negotiating and working with all kinds of contracts: contracts between the agency and its clients (representation agreements), and contracts for the clients with their employers

Because I immediately realized that the components of being a top talent agent reflected and were in perfect harmony with my *Clarifying Lists*, it was easy for me to turn down a position with a prestigious entertainment and sports law firm, and instead work for William Morris—even though the law firm would have paid me twice what my starting salary would be at William Morris. My belief was that if I love what I do and I am great at it, enough money would follow. About two years later, when I was assigned to significantly expand the William Morris local-news department, and when I subsequently left the agency to start my own firm, the major *Clarifying List* criterion of being an entrepreneur was also satisfied.

From the day that I began working at William Morris and throughout my agenting/entrepreneur career, I have been exhilarated, challenged, fulfilled . . . and yes, successful. Why? Because what I do effectively makes the most of my skills, assets, and passions. It truly is—and always has been—a tremendously rewarding niche.

The first step here is to take the requisite time to identify the things that you are good at and the things that you love or like to do or would love or like to do, as well as the things that you do *not* want to do or like to do.

One additional point. I am by no means saying that everything that you do in your job is going to be exciting or fun. We all must perform tasks that are tedious, boring, and unpleasant as a means to attaining a coveted, successful end. For example, being disciplined and delaying gratification at the appropriate times are part and parcel of the most rewarding careers. However, if your overall profession or the *Goals* that you seek to attain in your profession aren't exciting, challenging, or fulfilling, then you're going to be spending a great deal of your precious life feeling frustrated, unhappy, and empty. This is not a physically or emotionally healthy state of affairs—and you would do well to make some beneficial changes.

Let's focus a bit more on the process of compiling your *Clarifying List*. In 2008, I counseled "Danielle," who feared losing her livelihood, happiness, and professional passion as a result of the downturn in the economy and her father pressuring her to seek job security at the clear expense of job satisfaction. By her (and our) exploring and identifying her *Goals* and *Dreams*, we unearthed a great new employment option, which she explored and ultimately secured. Here is a bit more about Danielle and the relevant portions of our discussions:

Danielle was a forty-five-year-old single mom with a fifteen-year-old son, Patrick. A few years earlier, Danielle and her husband, Ed, separated. Allegedly, Ed had been out of work prior to the separation. This resulted in a major diminution of income that severely drained the couple's savings. During this time, the family lived on Danielle's income as a real estate broker.

Danielle was a bright and savvy individual who had always been driven to excel professionally. Upon her separation from Ed, Danielle ramped up her real estate business, and for the first year and a half, selling homes was relatively lucrative for her. But when the 2008 recession hit and sales came to a near standstill, Danielle's father implored her to "get out of real estate and find a job in a stable company that can give you and Patrick the guaranteed income and job security you need."

Sometime thereafter, I received a call from Danielle, who said, "Ken, I'm panicked and scared to death! I've lost nearly half of my

401K savings, and I'm not selling any houses. My dad's all over me to bag the real estate, because I'm totally responsible for my son's support. If I don't pay for his schooling, no one will. My dad wants me to take a boring corporate job. For the first time in my life, I'm really terrified! I feel like I'm being forced to make a snap decision, and I can't think straight. My dad called a couple of his corporate buddies and asked them as a favor to please find a position for me. I have interviews with them next week. But I know I'll hate the jobs! I've worked so hard to build up my real estate business. I hate to leave it all behind. You're the decision-making guru. What do I do?"

I responded to Danielle in the following way: "Okay. Let's relax and think this out clearly and carefully. Often, when you're overcome by fear or panic and have to make a decision, one of two things happens: You're frozen by your fear, so you can't or don't think or act rationally; or, you react without thinking clearly by acting inappropriately or in a self-sabotaging manner.

"But you aren't going to do either! Let me ask you some questions so that we can make a *Clarifying List*, and *you* can then figure this out. First of all, I'm gathering that what you want, above all else, is to continue to earn your living running your real estate business and helping your clients buy and sell homes. Is this correct?"

"Absolutely, *yes! That's* what I want!"

"Okay, you have now identified what I call one of your *Big-Picture Goals*. Obviously, one of your *Dreams* is to love what you do and adequately support your son and yourself."

Danielle then responded that if she didn't have the awesome, sole responsibility of making sure that her son was taken care of, she would stay in real estate and "risk it," but she believed that she couldn't take that chance under the circumstances.

I then asked, "So, in your sound, reasonable judgment, is there *any* way you see yourself doing enough real estate business in the foreseeable future to support you and your son?"

"No, I don't," she responded sadly.

"All right. Just your knowing that valuable information is both tremendously clarifying and a gift. Let's keep going, Danielle. Tell me more about where your professional passions lie."

"Well, I love real estate. But, you know, I grew up in the television-production business, because of my grandfather. I loved that, too. But when I had Patrick, I had to be home much more, so I left TV production. That was about fifteen years ago. It's been a while."

"Okay! You now have unearthed another *Goal*. You loved being in the television-production industry. Great! What facet of it excited you the most?"

"Sales. Selling shows to local station managers around the country. I loved being involved with the individuals who created the shows, as well as with the producers who gave the shows life. I *really* loved going around the country and explaining to the local station managers why they should buy *our* show! I'd always come up with novel sales approaches. Even more than the shows, I just loved being with smart, interesting people."

As Danielle answered this last question, you could see her light up.

I continued, "Great! Now tell me why you love the real estate business so much."

"I love working with people. I love looking at and marketing homes. I get a real thrill when I put people in homes they love. I'm a born marketer!"

"Danielle, we have now identified three more of your *Goals*. Let's begin to make your *Clarifying List*:

1. First and foremost, you love working with and being around *people*.

2. You love and have great talent in marketing.

3. It appears that you won't be happy or thrive in a structured office job not centered around dealing with people."

Danielle enthusiastically responded, "You got it!" Her demeanor continued to brighten, as she saw the progress we were making and the positives that could flow from our discussions.

I continued, "Any other *Goals* you can think of?"

"I want to do something that I love and can stay in for a long time. I feel that way about real estate. I'm great when I'm passionate about something. Then I'm engaged and I'll work like crazy! With no man in my life, I *really* want to love what I do professionally. You know, real estate got me out and meeting all sorts of wonderful people. I love that!"

"So," I continued, "what *don't* you want?"

"A job I don't care about in a field I have no interest in. But my dad is telling me that I *must* make a move now, even if I work for a bank. Oh my God, I *hate* the thought!"

"All right! It's time to make a more complete *Clarifying List*." I proceeded to write down her priorities, as I saw them:

1. To be a loving and financially responsible mother to Patrick

2. To do something you're passionate about

3. To not be one of those individuals who settles, simply because they're too lazy or afraid to seek out and secure what they truly want

4. To work with interesting people and use your great marketing skills

5. To have a career that allows you to spend enough time with Patrick

6. To keep your real estate business, if possible

7. If your real estate business isn't viable at this point, to return to the television-production industry

8. To have a career with longevity

"How's our *List?*" I asked.

"I love it! Right on target."

"Then let's go ahead and explore three concurrent or parallel choreographies, as time for you is of the essence. Since staying in real estate is a top *Goal*, is there any avenue you haven't yet explored that can keep you afloat in your chosen field? I know the economy's terrible, but certain unexpected conditions often create new niches. Is there any new niche out there that you can fill?"

Danielle thoughtfully responded, "Well, there *is* an opportunity for the people with expendable income to buy homes as investments at rock-bottom prices. It's far safer than putting their money in today's stock market."

"It sounds right to me. How much money do you have saved up?"

"About enough to support us for a year."

"Good. Our first choreography is for you to figure out the feasibility of refocusing your real estate business on bringing individuals with expendable income attractive investment properties. You've always dealt with an upscale clientele; hopefully, they're into having you find some sound investments for them. Do your homework and see if you can make a go of it."

"I *love* that idea!"

"At the same time, our second choreography is to have you call all of your contacts in the television-production arena. Maybe there's a position at one of these companies that can take advantage of your gifts. If there is, you can put your real estate business on hold until conditions are better. But who knows, maybe you'll have a long-term career in production!"

"I'm so excited, Ken. I feel so much better already. A little hope is a great thing! Seriously, thank you."

"You're welcome, Danielle, but as I always say, 'Without the right choreography steps, hope alone won't take you to the promised land!'"

"You're so right! Now, what do I do about the meetings my dad has set up for me?"

"That's your third choreography. Go to them. See what happens. You never know. But put the majority of your time, energy, and brilliance into seeing if you can create a new real estate niche for yourself, and spend the rest of your time landing meetings and interviewing with production companies."

"I'm ecstatic, Ken. We now have a crystal-clear game plan, a vision!"

"Remember the song we heard years ago, 'I can see clearly now, the rain is gone'? Well, with the right choreographies come clarity, direction, and calm. No more panic!"

"I can see and think clearly now. Yay!"

"Okay, time to get started doing your real estate research and setting up production-company interviews. Give it all you've got!"

"You've got it, Chief! I'll call you with my progress."

"Sounds great!"

Fortunately for Danielle, within four weeks, three self-enhancing events took place:

1. Her research and best judgment told her that being involved in any form of real estate business at such a precarious time would be too risky, given both the circumstances and her very real financial obligations. Once again, learning what you *don't* want or *shouldn't* do is a highly beneficial Career Choreography step.

2. Danielle interviewed for and was offered a newly created position in affiliate sales for a major production company. With tremendous excitement and gratitude, she accepted the offer.

3. She never had to seriously consider taking the corporate jobs that her father made her feel as if she had to take.

Obviously, not every set of choreographies will work out as neatly as it did for Danielle. But the concept to remember here is that by carefully and honestly compiling her *Clarifying List*, Danielle came up with a new, exciting employment option: becoming a television-production executive.[5]

One more story about how to identify your *Goals* and *Dreams* involves "Sarah."

The other day, a longtime client sought my counsel, as her daughter Sarah, who was going to be a college freshman, was contemplating possible career paths and what courses she might want to enroll in. Essentially, Sarah wanted to discuss possible career ideas.

After chatting with Sarah for a bit, I asked her what her *Dreams* were. She said she wanted to work in some way with Down syndrome children or be an elementary school teacher. Sarah obviously wanted to devote her career to helping children—possibly in the special-needs arena.

Our next step was to compose a *Clarifying List*. I asked her to write down what her passions and hobbies were, what was important to her, and what she didn't want to do professionally. Here's what Sarah wrote:

1. I love working with children, preferably between the ages of five and thirteen.

---

5   We will revisit the case of Danielle when we discuss "Fear Paralysis" in Chapter 29.

2. I would very much like to work with children in some way who have Down syndrome or other special needs.

3. I can't wait to be a mom! It's what I was born to do, and I want to be the very best mom possible.

4. I see myself as an elementary school teacher, but I also want to be a stay-at-home mom, so I'm not sure how that would work. I'm in conflict, because I feel that my wanting to be a stay-at-home mom won't allow me to pursue my professional *Dreams*. It's a big problem for me!

5. I'm a patient listener, and I enjoy helping people work out their problems.

6. Another passion of mine is music. I play the piano and the guitar. I don't know how I would use music in my career, but I'd love to find a way.

7. I also love playing soccer. I've played it since I was five.

We now had a very telling *Clarifying List* from which to work. Obviously, Sarah is an insightful and analytical young woman. From all indications, she had given her career aspirations a great deal of thought prior to our speaking. After listening to her a little more and hearing how she enjoys helping her friends solve their problems, I hit upon what I thought was a really interesting potential choreography for Sarah to consider.

Because her *Dream* is to work with special-needs children, why not become a psychologist for or some sort of counselor of special-needs children? This profession would take full advantage of Sarah's obvious excellent listening, intuitive, and counseling gifts, as well as her deep desire to help children. How wonderfully rewarding, and heart-and-soul nourishing for everyone involved! She could have her practice at her home or at a nearby office, so that she could make her own hours, and thereby be the stellar mom she so wants to be. Sarah can also use her piano and guitar playing as a form of music therapy with the children she counsels as a means to draw them out and bring the joy of music to them.

When I shared my career idea with Sarah, she loved it, as it seemed to allow her to follow all of her passions and meet all of her needs. She now had a direction and a key first step in her Career Choreography, which was to take the courses that would enable her to one day work with special-needs children. I'm thrilled for Sarah and for all of the fortunate children who will one day get to work with her.

Once you have identified your *Goals* and/or *Dreams* and made a *Clarifying List*, you can then narrow down and better pinpoint the type of work that will most likely satisfy your *Clarifying Criteria* and thereby make your heart sing!

One last, but crucially important point. When identifying your *Goals, Dreams*, and *Clarifying Criteria*, always be aware of this reality: As you grow, and have new and diverse experiences, your *Goals, Dreams*, and values will change as well. Therefore, your *Clarifying Lists* and choreographies will have to be reworked from time to time.

For example, I cannot tell you how many times friends and colleagues of mine thought their *Dream* was to become an attorney. But after attending law school or practicing law, their initial perceptions of this profession radically changed. As a result, some individuals left the field completely. Other attorneys, including me, no longer practice law as their main diet, but instead, now use some element of their legal training as part of a different profession from which they derive far more fulfillment. In either case, once a transformation in career *Goals* or values takes place, an amended or a totally new *Clarifying List* and choreography must be constructed.

An integral part of being an effective choreographer is that you regularly take the requisite time to explore your feelings in order to see if changes in your values, *Goals*, and *Dreams* have occurred. If so, your mission is to find out what your new values, motivations, *Goals*, and *Dreams* are. It can also be highly beneficial to try to understand why these changes have taken place. With this knowledge, you can then construct the most current and effective choreographies. You may want to visualize your role here as similar to that of a heart monitor, in that a heart monitor tracks and identifies changes in one's heart condition. Your objective, much like a heart monitor, is to continually study your heart of heart's values, *Goals*, and *Dreams* as they change.

Now that we have discussed the first step in your choreography—identifying your *Goals* and *Dreams*—let's explore your second step: identifying where you are today—or where you are starting from.

In preparation for the next chapter, please take time to think about and honestly assess where you are now. One way to accomplish this is to identify what your strengths, skills, and assets are, and what you need to experience, learn, develop, or improve upon in order to put yourself in the very best position to attain your *Goals* and *Dreams*.

When you do this, always take into account the current conditions and societal challenges. For example, in the case of Danielle, she had to factor our economic downturn into her thinking and plans. Similarly, you may be well served to consider how current economic and societal realities impact your choreography. Remember, honesty and nondefensive exploration are key concepts here.

WHERE ARE YOU TODAY?

The second step in your choreography process is to clearly identify and acknowledge where you currently stand professionally. You can accomplish this by asking the following questions:

1. What are my *Dreams* and *Goals* that I identified in Chapter 4?

2. What is the current state of my career, job, or position?

3. What are my specific skills and talents, as well as the life, work, and educational experiences that I have had that make up the package of who I am today?

4. Taking into account what my *Dreams* and *Goals* are and what my talents and experiences are, moving forward, what skills do I need to develop, and what experiences—educational or otherwise—do I need to have in order to put myself in the very best position to attain my professional *Goals* and live my career *Dreams*?

5. What is the current state of the economy in the country, in my business or the business that I aspire to enter into, and for me personally? Will the state of the economy in any of these areas impact or alter the choreography that I craft?

It is essential that you look at where you are professionally with an objective set of eyes, not through rose-colored glasses that make you feel better about your current lot in life. Additionally, don't obfuscate the truth by denying or repressing hard-to-face, uncomfortable, or depressing facts or circumstances. You must come at this process like a scientist, as you want to work with pure, accurate data only. It will be the truth that will set you free to be the most effective choreographer possible.

Take Danielle in the last chapter. She was completely truthful with me when she shared the following:

1. She was nearly paralyzed by fear because she thought she would have to leave her real estate business and take a job at a bank.

2. She realized there was no way during the economic downturn that she could support her son and herself with the real estate business that she had proudly created and nurtured over the past fifteen years, and so she would have to leave it.

3. She would sacrifice her professional happiness in order to support her son and herself.

4. With no partner in her life, her job satisfaction was especially important to her.

5. Optimally, she would love a sales position in television or real estate that would get her out of the office and working with interesting people.

Because Danielle was able to supply me and herself with an honest, accurate assessment, she was able to identify where she currently was and what her challenges and *Goals* were, thereby giving us the information we needed to craft her hugely successful choreography.

When assessing where you are today, be honest, accurate, insightful, and objective. By doing this, you give yourself the best chance to craft your most effective and success-evoking choreographies.

You must also make an honest assessment about what skills and experiences you need in order to grow, or else you may well not construct the necessary steps that will enable you to develop these much-needed skills and have these all-important foundation-building experiences. Additionally, if you lack the requisite knowledge and honed instincts, you will have a shoddy foundation, which could lead you to suffer future heart-crushing, crash-and-burn disappointments or disasters. Trust me, I've seen plenty of them during my career, and they almost all come about because the affected individuals never developed the goods to go the distance and put themselves in the best position to achieve their *Goals* or their *Dreams*, or to maintain them over the long term. Instead, they and their careers lay strewn by the wayside, in the dark and dank alley of disappointment and despair.

A perfect example of this crash-and-burn scenario comes to us in the form of "Tom," who was the star quarterback of his college football team and a hero in his small hometown. Upon his graduation, a local manufacturing company put him in an executive position without giving him any training.

Because of Tom's local popularity, for the first year after graduation he was able to bring clients into the firm based solely upon his successful football career and good looks. As a result, Tom didn't deem it necessary to arm himself with a working knowledge of the products his company manufactured, or the company's basic inner workings and financial underpinnings. He felt that he didn't have to, as he became intoxicated by how seemingly easy it was to initially attract and secure new business.

However, two years later, the company folded, and he and his

wife left town so she could pursue a more lucrative and challenging position. Much to Tom's surprise, he wasn't extended any offers
from the companies he interviewed with in their new city. When he
finally landed a position that was far less prestigious than the one
that he had held in his hometown, he was fired months later. Why
the dramatic lack of success? Because he never devoted the time
or energy to develop the requisite skills to be a knowledgeable and
effective employee. His hometown popularity and good looks meant
little in his new position, as he lacked a solid skill set and mindset
foundation in order to succeed. As a result, he never amounted to
anything and was relegated to suffering through a career filled with
frustration and bitterness.

"Ray" was a Latino reporter working in a small town. Because
he was extremely talented and a sought-after person of color to boot,
he received many offers, including one to report in Chicago—a
top-three-sized market. Because Ray's *Dream* was to be both an
anchor and a reporter in a large market, taking this position, which
only included reporting, was not a constructive next step in Ray's
Career Choreography.

The logical and constructive career step here would have been
for Ray to be disciplined and forgo the Chicago opportunity and
take the time to find a position at which he could develop *both* his
anchoring and reporting skills. However, the allure and immediate
ego gratification of moving to a much larger market for a seemingly
huge raise led Ray to accept a five-year reporter contract in Chicago.
He did this hoping that once he was in Chicago and had established
himself as a top reporter, he could then learn how to anchor there.
But by not respecting the appropriate Career Choreography strategies, Ray made a tragic career misstep.

During the next five years—prime learning and developing
years for Ray—he anchored only once. And on that occasion, he

appeared to be so inexperienced and unpolished—when compared with other Chicago anchors who had anchored for years in smaller markets before coming to Chicago—that Ray was never again assigned an anchoring opportunity at the Chicago station.

Toward the conclusion of his five-year stint, Ray's agent sent out demo tapes all over the country, hoping that Ray could be hired as an anchor somewhere else. Unfortunately for Ray, there were no takers. Obviously, relying on hope alone wasn't enough. Discouraged and resigned to his fate, Ray entered into another long-term reporter contract with his Chicago station. This step significantly decreased the chances that Ray would ever attain his *Dream* of securing a prime anchor position in a large market.

Ray is an example of someone who didn't follow the logical and constructive Career Choreography of developing a solid foundation of anchoring, as well as reporting skills in his chosen field. He paid—and continues to pay—dearly for it.

Unlike Ray, Rob Schmitt, who is currently an anchor and correspondent for the Newsmax network, exercised appropriate discipline when he crafted and began his choreography, and thereby followed the correct order of Career Choreography steps.

Years ago, I found Rob as an anchor and reporter in the Redding, California, market. Because of his obvious on-air gifts, I was able to secure major interest for Rob to make a meteoric rise to a New York City or a Chicago station as a reporter, with no anchoring. Similar to Ray, Rob would have received a massive pay raise and an intoxicating ego boost if he had accepted one of those positions. However, Rob and I both agreed that because Rob's *Dream* was to be a network weekday anchor and correspondent, taking a reporter position in New York City or Chicago was *not* the right next move. So he wisely declined both offers. A couple of weeks later, Rob received an offer to be a weekend anchor and reporter in Miami, which is one of the top news markets in the country. In this position, Rob could develop *both* his anchoring and reporting skills. And although Rob didn't receive as big of a salary in Miami as he would have in New York City or Chicago, he sagely delayed the immediate gratification of a substantial pay increase for a much bigger payday down the line as a network or local weekday anchor.

Rob accepted the Miami position and, two years later, moved to Los Angeles, the country's second largest market, as an anchor and reporter, then to New York City, the number-one market, in the same position. Throughout his choreography, Rob polished both his anchoring and reportorial skills, which prepared him for his next major position as a weekday anchor and correspondent for the Fox News Channel. As this book is being published, Rob is living his *Dream*, as he will soon host his own weeknight news program on Newsmax.

And yes, the results of Rob's discipline and delayed gratification were more than worth the wait.

Similarly, I applaud national newscasters Robin Meade, Liz Claman, Ana Cabrera, Diane Macedo, Shepard Smith, Katie Couric, and Megyn Kelly. All of these top-drawer anchors/hosts paid their dues as reporters before ascending to the far more lucrative and visible anchor desk or host chair. Practicing appropriate discipline is a Career Choreography staple.

Nationally acclaimed hosts such as Mario Lopez and Nancy O'Dell (former *Entertainment Tonight* host), whose choreographies we'll study in upcoming chapters, were honest and nondefensive in their assessments of where they were, and where and how they needed to grow, when they constructed their choreographies. They then took the necessary constructive steps to shore up their lack of experience in important areas. As a result, they both attained their *Dreams* of being national hosts.

So, when making your Step 2 assessments, do your best to identify whatever is necessary for you to develop a rock-solid skill-set foundation. Nothing is more constructive or self-enhancing than developing the requisite knowledge, skills, and honed instincts in whatever endeavor you pursue. If you possess these assets, not only will you in all likelihood excel at whatever you do, but you will also enjoy the process and the rewards so much more—as it's truly exhilarating to be amazing at what you do!

When counseling my clients about facing their weaknesses, or résumé shortcomings, I explain that it is essential for them not to ignore skills they need to work on or experiences that they need to have. Additionally, I've seen individuals engage in destructive rationalizations such as lying to themselves as to why they haven't succeeded in the past. They concoct excuses such as blaming others or unfavorable events or circumstances if they fail or don't succeed in a given endeavor. These individuals become so adept at hiding the truth from themselves that they fail to see how, time after time, their flawed thinking and actions are actually to blame for their lack of growth. Ultimately, they fail to identify and correct any problems.

This state of affairs is not only frustrating and sad for these defensive individuals but also self-sabotaging and toxic! If you want to grow, be successful, and achieve your most cherished *Goals*, you must be open to seeing your shortcomings so you can construct the steps that will help you eliminate any holes or flaws. One means of developing into a great choreographer is to engage in, and even relish, the non-strength identification process on a regular basis so that you can turn weaknesses into strengths and assets. As a choreographer, strive to be consistently great! Equip yourself with the strongest non-flawed foundation possible. On the other end of the spectrum, it is also important to be aware of and take full advantage of your strengths and assets when constructing your choreographies. We will discuss this topic in later chapters.

Before moving on, take time to think about whether you are truly open and honest with yourself when identifying and assessing your strengths, weaknesses, and necessary areas of growth. Examine whether defensive thinking has prevented you in the past from recognizing that important pursuits have not turned out as planned or hoped for because of your ineffective or destructive patterns of thinking or behavior. Always remember, "hindsight is 20/20" only if upon later review of your misstep, you objectively identify and assess how you went wrong or could have acted in a more enhancing manner. It's critical to your growth that you are truthful with your evaluations.

In connection with the upcoming choreography case studies, please be aware that all the steps we will discuss were thoughtfully calculated and consciously taken so as to put the percentages heavily in the *choreographer's* favor that he or she would achieve their desired career *Goals*. Once again, let's keep in mind the 8 Cs of Career Choreography Success:

Choreograph your Career by Consistently implementing Conscious, Constructive, success-evoking Choices, made with Cognitive Clarity.

Chapters 6 and 7 illustrate how a logical and constructive choreography leads to attaining coveted *Goals* and *Dreams*. We'll examine two different broadcasting Career Choreographies—those of Nancy O'Dell and "Christina Guardado."

First, a bit of background for these case studies. Most television newscasters begin their careers in small cities or markets, where they are paid very little. And in turn, little in the way of experience and polish is expected of them. It is at these jobs that young on-air individuals can make their beginners' mistakes and hopefully learn, develop, and grow. These positions, ideally, provide individuals with opportunities to write, gather information, and develop the skills of effectively reporting taped (prerecorded) pieces and doing live reports. All of these skills build an invaluable foundation for future jobs in larger and more challenging markets.

Although the first two case studies come from the field of broadcasting, the steps and strategies identified and discussed apply to any professional pursuit. Many of the steps and strategies taken and implemented by Nancy and Christina will be referred to throughout the remainder of this book. So, absorb them—be a sponge!

THE SOFT
CHOREOGRAPHY AND
THE SOFT-CONCURRENT
CHOREOGRAPHY

The Soft Choreography is a set of steps that will lay the foundation for you to choose, at a later time, the direction in which you want your career to go. This type of choreography is appropriate for individuals who desire to get the requisite training and experience to pursue two or more potential career options. At some point in the future, when they identify where their real passions lie, they can then make an informed, specific career choice.

For example, I know a number of individuals who started out as business-affairs-department attorneys for major theatrical agencies. Many of these individuals weren't sure whether they ultimately wanted to be career entertainment attorneys or, after spending a few years being trained in entertainment-agency contract law, they wanted to pursue a career as a theatrical agent, manager, or producer. Having a thorough entertainment-law background equipped them to be successful in all of these positions.

In my case, I eventually chose the agent route. Others stayed as business-affairs attorneys at their agencies or joined private law firms. Different results, but with one thing in common: By opting to implement a Soft Choreography, we were able to keep our career options open until we were ready to identify which career course best suited our unique skill sets, values, and passions.

I implemented a Soft Choreography when I attended law school. I had no idea if I wanted to practice law as a profession, but I knew that being educated as an attorney and learning how to think like one would prepare me for any field that I would later choose to pursue.

One of my associates took his Soft Choreography a couple of steps further. After working as a business-affairs attorney for three years, he became a motion-picture agent. However, he still wasn't certain that being a film agent was his ultimate calling. He wondered, "Maybe, being a major motion-picture producer *is*." As a result, he thoroughly learned the motion-picture business through representing feature-film writers, producers, and directors.

Once again, through a series of calculated Soft-Choreography steps, he thoroughly learned his business and made the requisite contacts. About five years later, with a wonderful future awaiting him in connection with whichever of the two courses he chose, he opted to become a film producer. Because he knew his stuff and had a gift for identifying commercial and compelling film properties, he grew to enjoy huge success in the film-production world. You have in all likelihood watched and enjoyed a number of the blockbuster films that this individual has produced.

THE NANCY O'DELL
SOFT-CONCURRENT CHOREOGRAPHY

I discovered Nancy O'Dell, who has hosted *Access Hollywood* and most recently *Entertainment Tonight*, when she worked as a morning anchor and an investigative reporter in Charleston, South Carolina. Upon speaking with Nancy, I gleaned that her *Dream* would be to host a national entertainment program, such as *Entertainment Tonight*, which at the time was the only major entertainment show of its kind. However, at the time, she was also interested in hosting a national news show, such as *Today*, *Good Morning America*, or *CBS Morning News*. We structured a Soft-Concurrent Choreography so that Nancy could eventually host national shows in *either* entertainment or news, thus leaving both options wide open for the future.

There is an important distinction to make between the Soft Choreography of the business-affairs attorneys mentioned earlier and Nancy's Soft-Concurrent Choreography. In the case of the attorneys, there was one choreography used to train and prepare them to be business-affairs attorneys, talent agents, film producers, or private-practice attorneys. That single choreography, which consisted of entertainment legal training and related experiences, allowed these individuals to choose—and later, successfully pursue—any of the aforementioned careers.

In Nancy's case, she pursued choreographies in both hard news and entertainment news at the same time, so as to leave her options wide open.

The result is the same in both examples—but with two different forms of the flexible choreography. Let's continue with Nancy's story.

When I began to send out demo tapes of Nancy's on-air Charleston work, we received interest from various local-news stations across the country, as well as from the E! entertainment network—which wanted Nancy to host one of its entertainment-news shows. Receiving interest from a prestigious—but relatively new—national cable network such as E! was very alluring, and for some, would have been intoxicating.

As we did with all potential employment opportunities, Nancy and I discussed the pros and cons of working for E! at such an early stage in her career. My counsel was for her to forgo the E! opportunity, because I firmly felt that it was the wrong step in her particular choreography. I believed that no matter whether Nancy aspired to host a national entertainment show or anchor a news program, she first needed to work for at least one more local station, in a top news market, in order to continue to hone her live news reporting and interviewing skills. This was an essential developmental step for her. I also saw two major drawbacks with the E! show Nancy would host. First, it was taped, so there would be no live reporting, hosting, or interviewing experiences from which Nancy could continue to grow. Second, if she hosted an entertainment show for E!, she would have lost the major-market local-news experience that a national news program such as the *Today* show would require. It was way too early in Nancy's budding career for her to put all her career eggs in the option-limiting, taped-entertainment television basket.

Nancy agreed with my Career Choreography perspective. She delayed the immediate gratification of accepting the position at E! and went to a news station in Miami, where she distinguished herself as both an evening anchor and a reporter. Most important, she developed the necessary live skills in order to become a viable candidate for any national news or entertainment position.

As time passed, Nancy's career path became more clearly defined— she was moving intellectually and emotionally toward hosting a national entertainment show. Therefore, the next steps in her choreography were to get her some entertainment/pop-culture reporting assignments in Miami with which to market her, and then move her out of hard news and into the entertainment arena. We soon found the right opportunity. Nancy joined Fox as a national entertainment reporter—a move we both felt would bring her a step closer to her

Goal of hosting a national entertainment show. About a year later, NBC and Fox teamed up to produce *Access Hollywood*, which would be a national, five-days-a-week entertainment show, and Nancy became its weekend host, and then its weekday host. Interestingly, we were told that one of the reasons Nancy was given the position over others was because she had excellent live skills, so her news stint in Miami paid off big-time! Years later, Nancy lived her ultimate *Dream*, as she became the co-host of *Entertainment Tonight*.

THE SOFT-CHOREOGRAPHY REVIEW

1. In Nancy's case, she initially identified her two *Dreams* of hosting a national entertainment show and a national morning news/interview program.

2. She developed solid foundations in *both* entertainment and news so that she would one day have the option to pursue either *Dream*—or possibly both, at different times in her career.

3. With time came career clarity, as Nancy recognized that she was passionate about attaining her *Dream* of being a host of a major entertainment show.

4. The steps that constitute an effective Soft Choreography are designed to equip you with the necessary training, experience, knowledge, and honed instincts so that, when the timing is appropriate, you have the flexibility to choose which of a *number of career options* is the most suitable for and attractive to you.

THE HARD CHOREOGRAPHY

The Hard Choreography is for individuals who know exactly what they want. In essence, you take "dead aim" at the *Dream* that you want to live and then devise the steps that will give you the experiences, training, knowledge, and honed instincts to attain your *Goal* or *Dream*. For instance, if you are clear about your *Goal* or *Dream*—whether it's to become a doctor, carpenter, makeup artist, business owner, or what have you—you can then devise a uniquely personal and effective Hard Choreography that will put the percentages heavily in your favor that you will secure what you want. Whereas the Soft Choreography is flexible and designed to allow you to leave your career options open, the Hard Choreography is singularly focused on achieving a clearly defined *Goal*, or set of *Goals*, or *Dream*.

For example, individuals who want to be dancers, gymnasts, ice skaters, or the most accomplished painters, writers, or professional athletes are often singularly focused on achieving greatness in their identified arena—to the exclusion of allowing themselves to take advantage of other varied, nonrelated activities. They know what they want. They can see it, and they hunger for it. For these individuals in particular, the right personally appropriate Hard Choreography may well help them achieve their *Dreams*.

However, it is always important to keep in mind that during the course of implementing any Hard Choreography, you can at any point modify your originally conceived choreography steps in order to make them more effective. Even with a Hard Choreography, there is always room for flexibility and change. The reason we refer to this form of choreography as "hard" is because the *Goal* or *Dream* that you aspire to attain has been set in stone—but not necessarily the means.

THE "CHRISTINA GUARDADO" HARD CHOREOGRAPHY

Prior to my representing Christina, I perceived her to be beating out all of my clients for jobs that were incorrect *for her*. My thought process was that a great deal of Christina's early work was on tape— which can be shot over and over again until it is perfect. But the problem with perfect is that it's often plastic. And one of the things that makes Christina so exceptional is that she is great in a live format. She is also an exceedingly bright, genuine, spontaneous, funny, and quick-witted host and interviewer, not to mention a highly intuitive and respectful listener. So the taped and tightly scripted positions that she had been accepting didn't play to or showcase her strengths.

One day, I saw Christina conduct an outstanding live interview, and I immediately called her with an interest in becoming her representative. The next day I flew to San Francisco and we met. At our lunch, I asked Christina, "What would make your heart sing?" After joking that she would like to get better ratings on her midday news show, she shared her heartfelt answer: "I'd like to host a major national morning show." To my mind, this was an attainable— although lofty—*Dream*, because most national morning shows feature live interviewing, which was one of Christina's strengths.

As I spoke a bit more with Christina, I realized that her true *Dream* position was to host one of the three major network morning shows. Okay, we had our one clearly defined *Dream*. The next step was to construct the most effective Hard Choreography possible. Part and parcel of doing this was to thoughtfully identify the skills and experiences that hosting a major network morning show required. In my mind, I listed the following:

1. A hard-news background

2. The ability to synthesize and analyze information and/or breaking news quickly

3. Extensive live interviewing experience in both hard-news and lighter-news (i.e., pop culture) contexts

4. The gravitas, credibility, and honed skill set to host a network morning show when a major hard-news story is breaking

5. The ability to be comfortable and to have fun with doing light interviews and segments

6. The ability to think quickly and effectively on one's feet

The aim of this *List* was to identify what skills Christina needed to develop and polish so she would be ready for a network morning-show hosting job if and when an opening occurred. Unquestionably, our next steps were to develop her hard-news skills and credentials, and then to identify which jobs and station assignments would most efficaciously help her develop those skills, as well as obtain the required news experience. I then told Christina that the optimal opportunity would be for her to one day anchor a news program such as the late afternoon newscast at her San Francisco station, where she would anchor the news as well as conduct daily live interviews.

Over the next few years, Christina took dead aim at her ultimate *Dream* by taking positions and requesting and accepting assignments that enabled her to attain the requisite experience to be a strong candidate to host a network morning show. With focused hard work on Christina's part, and some fortuitous timing, Christina was hired as a network weekend morning-show host and later lived her *Dream* of hosting a major network morning show. She in large part was able to accomplish this by constructively implementing her highly beneficial Hard Choreography.

THE HARD-CHOREOGRAPHY REVIEW

1. Identify your *Dream*.

2. Honestly and objectively identify the skills and experiences you need in order to put yourself in the strongest position to attain your *Dream*.

3. Construct a choreography that will enable you to attain the necessary skills and experiences to put the percentages heavily in your favor that you will live your *Dream*.

4. Wisely, creatively, and flexibly implement your Hard-Choreography steps.

MULTIPLE CHOREOGRAPHIES

It is rare when someone only has one career *Goal* or *Dream*, achieves it, and thereafter decides that no further *Goals* or *Dreams* remain to be fulfilled. More often, as individuals change and grow, they have many career *Goals* and *Dreams*—or, as they say, people have at least two career "acts." It makes sense that, with new and changing *Goals*, new or additional choreographies need to be created and implemented.

For example, I had a specific choreography for learning and successfully competing in both tennis and POP Tennis, being successful in both college and law school, being successful at the William Morris Agency, starting my own company, and, as I will discuss in a later chapter, navigating the national and international growth of POP Tennis.

As with all choreographies, the key is to devise personally effective steps so that you attain your *Goals* and derive fulfillment during the process.

Here is an example.

JACK LINDNER'S MULTIPLE CHOREOGRAPHIES

Choreography I—The Vertical Choreography

My dad, Jack, came to the United States from Poland as an adolescent, didn't speak any English, and needed to start working immediately to help his widowed mother support their family. To learn to speak English as soon as possible, he decided to spend time with American boys so he would be exposed to the English language and American culture.

During his teen years, Jack took various menial jobs to help his mother make ends meet. One day, while making a delivery to a department store, he was fascinated by the action and goings-on at that store. He saw how a well-dressed man seemed to be running things on the main floor that busy Saturday afternoon, and he learned that this individual was the merchandiser of the women's clothing department. When he asked friends how one could become a merchandiser, he was told that you start out in a training program, eventually become an associate buyer, then a buyer, and if you do well, a merchandiser, via a promotion. Upon hearing this, Jack's *Dream* was set. He wanted to become a merchandiser in a department store, just like the one to whom he had made the delivery.

Soon thereafter, my dad identified a major obstacle to his gaining admission into a buyer-trainee program—he didn't have the high-school education that the buyer-trainee program required. All he had were his passion to better himself, his creativity, his strong drive, and his innate skills.

After doing some homework, Jack decided that he would take an overnight job as a stock boy, just to get himself into the store. And once he became an employee, he would somehow find a way to learn as much as he could about all aspects of the department-store business—especially the buying and merchandising areas—so there wouldn't be anything that he didn't know about these subjects. His *Goal* was to more than make up and compensate for his lack of a formal education with his intimate knowledge of how this department store functioned.

Fortunately, my dad secured a job in the receiving room of the department store he coveted. Unfortunately, because of his overambitious behavior, he rubbed some supervisors the wrong way, as he showed them up by proving that they didn't truly know the prices of the goods that their stores were selling. As a direct result, he was quickly fired. A Career Choreography crisis? No, a valuable lesson! He realized he had to keep his burning desire to make good in check and to develop a demeanor that would foster harmonious working relationships.

So, a bit wounded but undaunted, my dad secured an overnight receiving-room position at another department store. This time he stayed and absorbed everything he could. Eventually, he was promoted to a better position in the receiving room and worked days, during which he would sometimes venture onto the main floor where all the action was—a place he still yearned to be.

As he walked around that floor, he carefully studied which women's fashions were selling and which weren't. While working in the receiving room, he also made careful mental notes as to how much the buyers paid for the goods from the manufacturers and how much his store sold these goods for (the markup). He also learned how many pieces of clothing the buyers would initially order and reorder in succession, and how quickly and how much of a reduction in the sales price his store would take if a particular style wasn't selling.

Then came the turning point in my dad's career. It was choreography *carpe diem*! On an early Saturday morning, when no buyers or merchandisers had yet made it onto the main floor, my dad happened to be there when a manufacturer came up to him. Assuming that my dad was a buyer (as my dad took care to make a good appearance), the manufacturer said that he had stopped by to see how his clothes were selling. Knowing that the manufacturer's goods were selling extremely well, my dad decided to seize the moment and use his extensive knowledge and good instincts to negotiate a deal to reorder hundreds of the two styles that he believed were that manufacturer's hottest sellers. Within fifteen minutes, the deal points had been worked out.

Three days later, when the goods came streaming in and then showed up on the floor, no one knew which buyer had ordered them—until the department merchandiser checked to see who had signed the order slip. When he discovered that no buyer, but rather a receiving-room clerk, had signed the order form, a furious merchandiser ordered my dad up to the store president's office to not only have my dad fired but also learn enough about the transaction so that he and the president could figure out a way to nullify it.

Once in the office, the merchandiser asked my dad how he had the "audacity" and the "stupidity" to order the goods. My dad took the opportunity to show all of his knowledge and insights. He knew how well the goods had been selling. He also knew what the current sportswear buyer had paid for them. My dad then explained that he was able to purchase the goods for *more than thirty percent less* than that buyer had paid for them, and if the store ran a sale for ten percent off the goods' current price, they'd make a killing! He ended by passionately saying, "I got the right goods, at the right time, at the right price, so I made the deal."

The merchandiser hated hearing that his buyer had paid too much for the goods. But the president loved my dad's command of the business and his chutzpah.

At the president's behest, the merchandiser begrudgingly followed my dad's marketing plan, and the following Saturday, the goods flew out of the store . . . at a huge profit. (Yay, Dad!)

Two days later, my dad was promoted to assistant buyer. In this instance, my dad was able to take a hugely worthwhile calculated risk, because he was so confident in his actions.

My dad continued to learn everything he could about the business by working extra hours, going to competitive stores and observing what was and wasn't selling there, and establishing strong relationships with manufacturers. Before he negotiated, he always did his homework. He also did all he could to stay ahead of every buying and manufacturing curve. What I learned from listening to my dad was that knowing what to buy, how much to buy, and how far to go in negotiations and the like required specific knowledge and honed instincts. By immersing himself in his business, he developed an extraordinary feel for all of its aspects, such that he became an invaluable asset to his employer (and a pain in the *ass-et* to insecure superiors).

In time, my dad was promoted from assistant buyer to buyer, to merchandiser, to vice president, to executive vice president of the chain of stores: a beautiful Horatio Alger story. Each time my dad achieved a *Goal*, he identified a new *Goal* and immediately set about designing a choreography with which to attain it. Throughout his career with this company, my dad was acutely aware that he didn't have the formal education that others with whom he was competing for jobs enjoyed. However, he more than made up for this non-strength with his knowledge of, instincts regarding, and passion for his job. He also became a legendary trainer of future buyers—two of whom, Ben Cammarata and Norman Ferber, went on to become chairman of the board of T.J. Maxx and Ross, respectively.

But at sixty-six years young, my dad was suddenly "retired" by his company.

Choreography II—The Horizontal Choreography

My dad was in no way ready to be put out to pasture. He felt he had much more that he could still contribute to another chain of stores. He just needed the opportunity. But, he wondered, who, in this youth-minded society, would give a sixty-six-year-old man a chance? Although my dad never admitted it, the emotional wind had been taken out of his sails.

However, he didn't become a career casualty. Instead, he once again became a Career Choreographer. He decided to take steps to put the percentages in his favor for getting back in the game by:

1. Staying in tip-top physical and mental shape. My dad had always exercised. Throughout his working life, he made sure to walk a mile or so, or swim, and get adequate rest each day. My dad's perspective was that no one wants to work with someone who looks, acts, or thinks old. So you must stay fit, dress neatly and well, and be ahead of the curve when it comes to knowing your business.

2. Proactively staying in touch with the manufacturers with whom he had done business and with whom he potentially would do business in the future.

3. Keeping in contact with potential employers.

4. Continuing to read whatever materials were available (e.g., *Women's Wear Daily*) in order to stay knowledgeable about and current with his business.

5. Maintaining a positive and constructive state of mind.

Unlike the vertical choreographies that preceded this one, I refer to this portion of my dad's choreography as "horizontal" because he implemented all of the steps at the same time, as opposed to one after another.

Then, one day, when my dad was sixty-nine, Ben Cammarata—a former buyer trainee—called to say that he had just started a new chain of stores called T.J. Maxx. When Ben inquired as to whether my dad would be interested in going back to work for "a couple of weeks" to train T.J. Maxx buyers the way he had trained buyers such as Ben years earlier, my dad was ecstatic and immediately accepted.

That "couple of weeks" turned into almost thirty years. During this time, my dad continued to implement his consistently successful horizontal choreography strategies of staying fit, dressing well, thinking young and progressively, and staying ahead of the curve and *relevant*, until he retired at ninety-eight years old.

Through the right choreographies, my dad, who started out with many strikes against him, had two wonderfully rewarding long-term careers. He also enjoyed consistent and sustained success.

9

THE STEP-BACK
CHOREOGRAPHY

I wholeheartedly believe that you often have to take a step back in order to take many rewarding steps forward. In certain situations, insightful Career Choreography mandates that you follow this strategy. To illustrate, let's discuss the case of the Sibila Vargas Step-Back Choreography.

When I first met Sibila, she was a producer at a New York City television station. Her *Goal* was to become an on-air news anchor or program host. Her *Dream* was to be a weeknight anchor in her hometown of New York City. After securing excellent entertainment host and reporter positions, she was hired by CNN as an entertainment correspondent and host, which was a huge opportunity and a great accomplishment. A wonderful thing about CNN is that it has the credibility to attract the top celebrities who, for the most part, are happy to be interviewed on such a well-respected national/international platform. All this was great for Sibila, until time passed, and she recognized that her true *Goal* was to leave the world of entertainment and become a major news anchor. Unfortunately, because she hadn't yet established her hard-news anchoring or reporting credentials, CNN understandably didn't give her the opportunity to anchor for them. As a result, Sibila found herself firmly *stuck* in a position that she no longer enjoyed or wanted.

So, with this insurmountable obstacle squarely in her path, Sibila and I decided that she needed to leave the prestigious national platform of CNN and go back to local news in order to begin her hard-news anchoring career. Essentially, she would take what could be perceived as a step back in order for her to secure the necessary anchor training so she could pursue her lofty *Dream* of becoming a weeknight anchor in New York City.

We found a position for Sibila in Houston as a hard-news, Monday-through-Friday anchor, and she was off and running. After three years, she secured a position as a Monday-through-Friday morning anchor in Los Angeles. Two years later, the general manager of the NBC station in New York City—her hometown—saw Sibila anchor while he was visiting L.A. He decided then and there that he wanted her to become his weekday six p.m. anchor with the legendary Chuck Scarborough. The general manager offered Sibila her *Dream* job at WNBC—which she gratefully accepted. She was soon promoted to be the five, six, and eleven p.m. weeknight anchor there, and Sibila was living her *Dream*!

All of these wonderful things were accomplished because Sibila wisely, and with great discipline, took a strategic career-path detour to develop the requisite anchoring skills and experience so that she could take gratifying steps forward.

THE JUMP-START
CHOREOGRAPHY

Feeling or being stuck, mired, plateaued, or frustrated in a position is common. In these instances, you may well need a jump-start! The Jump-Start Choreography is most often used when there doesn't appear to be a logical next step or set of steps in connection with your *current* choreography. Crafting an effective Jump-Start Choreography enables you to creatively begin a new plan or make a detour, to better equip you to attain specific new *Goals* and *Dreams*.

Years ago, I counseled a very bright, ambitious young woman, "Lisa," who was in the midst of developing a spray-tanning business. She didn't have much money to start it, but fortunately, someone she knew had a portable spray-tan machine that he no longer needed. He was willing to let her use the machine so she could start her business, with a very small down payment and a royalty payment for each spray tan that she gave. This form of a two-tiered payment structure allowed Lisa to get started with a minimal investment, so it was ideal.

When we first met, Lisa was thinking about moving to Los Angeles and expanding her business. After chatting with her and hearing her aspirations, I gave her a few potential Jump-Start Choreography steps:

1. Align yourself with and give spray tans at some of the high-end hotels in Beverly Hills. This will give you access to individuals who are willing to spend money while on their vacations, as well as to those who live in or frequent the Beverly Hills area. This can result in your attaining a high-end clientele and cachet.

2. Associate yourself with and give spray tans at upscale hair salons in Beverly Hills and other upscale areas for the same reasons.

3. Develop a high-end "concierge" tanning service in places such as Beverly Hills, Malibu, and the Pacific Palisades, where you can give customers spray tans in the comfort of their own homes and charge a top price.

4. Contact residential realtors in the Beverly Hills/L.A. area and offer them the following: When they sell or lease a home to someone, they will give the client a "present" of a spray tan at his or her new residence. As a result, two things are accomplished: The realtor builds goodwill with the client, and you get to give a gift to a person who may ultimately become a steady customer. In order to entice realtors, provide them with spray-tan gift certificates for clients at a deeply discounted price. You can then apply this strategy to other businesses as well, for example, by selling this service as a Christmas or holiday gift that companies can give to their employees.

These were steps for Lisa to jump-start her business by developing an attractive clientele—who will ideally become repeat customers. Once she had enough business to warrant it, she could hire others to give spray tans as well. That way, her income wasn't solely based on the spray tans that she gave. This is often called passive income, in that Lisa wasn't directly doing the work to earn the money.

I'm thrilled to report that Lisa's Jump-Start Choreography was a huge success in both Los Angeles and parts of Orange County.

Another example of a creative and highly effective Jump-Start Choreography involved my client Christina McLarty.

I found Christina at KTVT, the CBS-owned station in Dallas. Within a couple of months of our beginning to work together, an entertainment-reporter position opened up at KCBS, in Los Angeles. This was the perfect next choreography step in Christina's career, as this position would give her the big-market experience she needed. Additionally, almost all of the most important entertainment magazine shows (*Entertainment Tonight*, *Access Hollywood*, *Extra*) are based in L.A., as are most of the entertainment/programming executives, so she would receive incredible, high-echelon exposure there. With these thoughts in mind, I submitted Christina's work to KCBS, and fortunately, they hired her.

After she had been at KCBS for three years or so, Christina felt stagnant regarding her work assignments. It was time to make our next move, which was to secure a national entertainment position for her. The problem was, there seemed to be no appropriate position available. Christina felt as if she had plateaued and had no logical next position to secure. However, she soon came up with a brilliant jump-start idea that would put the percentages far more in her favor that she would attain her *Dream* of working for *Entertainment Tonight* (*ET*) or *The Insider*. This was her strategy: *ET* and *The Insider* are both CBS-owned and CBS-distributed shows—and they are located on the same lot as KCBS. So why not propose to KCBS management that Christina do a series of promotional reports about *ET* and *The Insider*? This series would feature in-depth interviews with *ET* and *Insider* executives, as well as with the shows' hosts. The brilliance of this Jump-Start Choreography was that it would give Christina meaningful contact with all of the *ET* and *Insider* executives (and they would see what an exceptionally talented person she was). Because this was great cross-promotion for two CBS-owned shows, which aired on KCBS, KCBS management approved Christina's doing the series.

As she had choreographed and envisioned, Christina hit the interviews out of the park. A few weeks later, she became a correspondent for *The Insider*, as they created a position just for her. Thereafter, she fulfilled her *Dream* by being hired as a correspondent and fill-in host by *Entertainment Tonight*. All of these career-making events occurred for Christina because she was able to come up with a creative means to initiate meaningful contact with a desired employer through her highly creative Jump-Start Choreography.

There is a Jump-Start Choreography for every endeavor. You just have to see the big picture, determine who benefits from different business relationships, and discover logical "fits," associations, partnerships, and affiliations. Then create an appropriate choreography that takes advantage of all of this knowledge.

Crafting an effective Jump-Start Choreography enables you to either creatively begin a new mini-choreography or make a choreography detour that will better equip you to attain your new *Goals* and *Dreams*.

MY POP TENNIS
CHOREOGRAPHY

To end this part of *Career Choreography*, I'd like to share a highly successful choreography[6] that I recently crafted and implemented to take a relatively unknown, local sport—paddle tennis—and transform it into a national and international sport in a relatively short time, with a pittance of money spent.

The backstory on paddle tennis is that it is a 120-year-old sport that was mostly played in small enclaves in New York City and Los Angeles. One of the biggest challenges to the sport's growth was that there were almost no national or international "official" 50 x 20 paddle tennis courts on which to play. So the sport's growth was basically nonexistent. Also, the sport of paddle tennis and its name were continually confused with that of sports such as platform paddle tennis (played on a platform, with wire mesh surrounding the court), pickleball, padel, beach tennis, and the like. So there was significant brand confusion should someone want to market the sport. As soon as I decided to grow paddle tennis, the first thing I thought was "What is the wisest choreography I can construct, knowing that

---

6   You can find your *Choreography List* in the appendix and download it at www.careerchoreography.com.

there are almost no paddle tennis courts in the U.S., and I have only a few thousand dollars to spend marketing the sport?"

Here is the choreography I created.

Step 1: Leo Ricagni needed a fresh new name so that paddle tennis would no longer be confused with platform paddle tennis and other sports. We came up with and adopted the name "POP Tennis" for our sport for many reasons: "POP" refers to being "popular," as in pop culture or pop entertainment. We wanted POP Tennis to be a sport of the people and a sport that everyone can play. Also, the tennis ball makes a popping sound when the POP Tennis racquet strikes it, so there is a double entendre. I trademarked both the name POP Tennis and an eye-catching POP Tennis logo.

Step 2: I called a meeting of about fifty major POP Tennis influencers and explained my choreography in order to secure their support and participation.

Step 3: We formed the United States POP Tennis Association, Inc., and became a 501(c)3 charitable organization.

Step 4: We created an exciting, informational website as our home base. The explicit goals for our site were to get people interested in playing POP Tennis and to answer any questions they might have.

Step 5: I called upon my extensive Los Angeles television news contacts, and all six Los Angeles stations aired positive stories and interviews about how fun and exhilarating it is to play POP Tennis. So our sport received major local exposure.

Step 6: I secured national exposure for POP Tennis by arranging for the *Today* show to do a wonderful live piece and set of interviews on POP Tennis. This major national exposure was game-changing! The publicity led to a number of news outlets doing stories on POP Tennis. For example, the Associated Press produced a great story on POP Tennis, which I am told ran in hundreds of cities around the world.

Step 7: My goal was to have POP Tennis be adopted by a major entity, much like the Women's National Basketball Association (WNBA) was adopted and supported by the National Basketball Association (NBA). Fortunately, this occurred when an executive from the United States Tennis Association (USTA) called me after watching the *Today* show POP Tennis piece. He suggested that we use the USTA's twenty-thousand-plus short tennis courts around the country to grow POP Tennis. We immediately seized this great idea and soon had the much-needed courts on which we could grow our sport nationally.

Step 8: We continued to arrange for local and national television, newspaper, magazine, and Internet exposure, and we hosted POP Tennis exhibitions and clinics across the country. Soon, sports facilities and venues from all over the world began contacting us to learn how they could bring POP Tennis to their clubs, parks, and cities.

Step 9: We changed the name of our organization to the International POP Tennis Association, Inc., to reflect the growing worldwide interest in and growth of our sport.

Step 10: We continue to grow our sport through multimedia exposure, exhibitions, and strategic alliances with supportive and nurturing organizations throughout the world.

The choreography steps continue!

The POP Tennis set of steps that I crafted is a straightforward Hard Choreography, and as I took dead aim at my *Goal*—

1. I identified the *Goal* I wanted to attain, which was to have POP Tennis played throughout the world.

2. I honestly assessed where I was starting from and the challenges I had to successfully meet: that POP Tennis was barely played anywhere in the U.S. and that there was a paucity of courts in the U.S. to play on, and none existed internationally.

3. I choreographed the most success-evoking set of steps with which to go from my starting point to my finish line.

It is truly gratifying to watch the substantial growth of POP Tennis in such a short amount of time—with a very small outlay of money. As I've shown in so many examples throughout this book, being a skillful choreographer can enable and empower you to accomplish truly amazing things!

Part II

Career Choreography Strategies to Attain Huge Success Throughout Your Career Journey

LEAD WITH YOUR STRENGTH

It has always been one of my *Dreams* to write self-help books—with at least one devoted to enabling foster children and other life-challenged children to make positive life choices, in spite of a lack of consistent love and caring that they oftentimes must endure and overcome. So about twenty years ago, I wrote a book on developing core confidence and feelings of high self-esteem in children so they would feel capable of making positive life choices for themselves and their futures.

The problem I encountered when I began marketing this book was that the executives in the publishing industry didn't perceive me as someone who had the credibility in the self-help or child-psychology areas to be an accepted author in these fields. These were valid points. So, I decided to go back to the drawing board and craft a choreography that would enable me to be successful in my pursuit.

Since my *Dream* was to be an author of self-help books, my first step was to become an author. In essence, I needed to get into "the club."

I employed a strategy I had successfully used time and time again with my clients: "Lead with your strength." This called for me to write a book in my field of expertise, so that my credibility wouldn't be called into question. So I led with my strength and wrote a book about broadcasting.

The next step was to employ another strategy I had previously used with great effectiveness: "When starting a new business or embarking on a new endeavor, try to identify an area that no one has ever tapped into before, or, if what I'm planning to do isn't new, I must either do it better than anyone else or differently and better than anyone else." In this instance, I needed to find a new market or an untapped niche in an already-established market.

My next step was to research what broadcasting books had already been published and what they focused on. I found an abundance of books that covered the history of broadcasting, and a plethora of memoirs written by recognizable broadcasters. What hadn't yet been written was a book about the psychology of broadcasting—or the real-life issues that broadcast journalists and aspiring broadcast journalists face when making decisions about their careers. Voilà!

This topic was perfect for two reasons. First, counseling budding and established newscasters, as well as program hosts, was what I did all day, every day, so I had the credibility and experience to write an impactful book that merited publication. Second, one of my strong interests since college has been the dynamics of decision making. So, by equipping broadcast journalists with everything that I know about successfully dealing with the day-to-day issues of broadcasting, I would empower them to make constructive and self-enhancing career and life decisions on their own. As a result, this book would help me accomplish three key, coveted goals:

1. It would help broadcasters throughout the country strategically develop their careers.

2. It would make me an author.

3. It would move me a step closer to being a self-help
   book author.

The next step was to either write an outline of my book or write the book itself. I opted to write the full book because I felt that since I had many unique insights to share, why not give the publishers a full blast of my expertise and credibility in this arena? I would leave nothing to the imagination or to chance!

My next move was to find a literary agent to market my proposed book, *The Psychology of Broadcasting*, to publishers. However, all the agents I contacted saw my book as a "trade" book and felt it was limited in scope and potential readership, and therefore the relatively meager commission they would make wasn't worth their time.

So circumstances necessitated a reconstruction of my choreography, in that I would not have an agent for this book. Instead, I went to various large bookstores, identified the limited number of companies that published broadcasting books, and contacted them myself.

The good news was that because I had a prestigious client list, the five publishers with which I made contact were interested in reading my manuscript. Three of them made offers to publish it. I chose the publisher with which I was most compatible, and my book was eventually published under the title of *Broadcasting Realities*. I was now a published author!

The feedback I received from broadcast journalists across the country was extremely positive and encouraging, as they said I was able to tap into how they were thinking and feeling, and provided what they needed to know about the business. I received a lot of thank-yous. Also, I was told consistently that the book's advice and strategies (called "News Tips") were applicable to all careers, not just to those of broadcast journalists. All of this was very gratifying, as I was enabling broadcasters and those aspiring to be on-air to grow.

About two years later, while I was giving a speech discussing the art of decision making, I found myself sharing some new thoughts, just as a comedian might go to a comedy club to try out some new material and see how the audience responds. On this day, I spoke about the awesome and often sabotaging impact that our emotions have on our life-choice making. Essentially, I explained that you can be the smartest person, with the wisest and most beneficial life strategies, but if you make decisions when you're angry, sad, or feel hurt, rejected, jealous, needy, hopeless, and the like, your best, rational judgment can be dismantled, and you can very likely make a diminishing or self-sabotaging decision. I then discussed my *7 Steps of Emotion Mastery*, which I had developed as a means for having the energy from your strongest emotions and your intellect (what you know or intuit) work in harmony in empowering you to make beneficial life choices that lead to success.

At the conclusion of my speech, a former *Oprah* show producer walked up to me and shared that she very much agreed with what I had said, in that it appeared as if I had found an effective way to enable individuals to make beneficial use of their potentially toxic emotions so they could make life choices that were consistent with their highest *Goals* and ideals. She ended our conversation by suggesting that I write a book about the process of *Emotion Mastery*, and that if I did, I could help a great many people. As we will discuss, a particle in motion can attract other highly valuable particles in motion. Thank goodness I took the time to make that speech and thereby meet that insightful producer!

I wound up taking that magnanimous producer's advice and immediately began writing. Five years later, I completed *Your Killer Emotions: The 7 Steps to Mastering the Toxic Emotions, Urges, and Impulses That Sabotage You.* I was told that *Your Killer Emotions* became both a Barnes & Noble and an Amazon best-seller;

additionally, the book has been published in a number of countries. In fact, just as I completed *Career Choreography*, the audio rights to *Your Killer Emotions* were licensed to China!

I am now living my *Dream* of being a self-help book author and speaker, and this has all become a rewarding reality by virtue of crafting the most success-evoking choreography possible. And the whole choreography was jump-started by my implementing the strategy of "lead with your strength," which was writing a book about the psychology of broadcasting, which was squarely in my wheelhouse.

For your review, here is my "How I can become a published author in the self-help arena" choreography:

1. I led with my obvious strength by deciding to write a book about broadcasting in order to establish myself as an author. This strategy got me off to a very positive start.

2. I found the right hook for the book.

3. I wrote the book.

4. I searched for a reputable literary agent.

5. After not being able to find an agent, I researched the companies that published broadcasting trade books and contacted them myself.

6. I chose a publisher.

7. *Broadcasting Realities* was published.

8. I started choreographing steps to make inroads into the self-help market.

9. I took the opportunity, when giving speeches, to discuss material that was broader than just broadcasting.

10. I gave a speech that led me to write a book about mastering one's emotions— *Your Killer Emotions: The 7 Steps to Mastering the Toxic Emotions, Urges, and Impulses That Sabotage You.*

11. I marketed this book on television, radio, social media, in print, and through public speaking.

12. I then wrote *Career Choreography.*

The self-help book choreography continues . . .

Once again, always keep in mind that there is a logical, constructive, and success-evoking choreography to achieve any *Goal*—whether it relates to your job, your career, or a hobby/pursuit.

Here's another example of the "lead with your strength" strategy. A few years ago, I was introduced to Lisa Dergan, a new client of our office. Upon meeting her, I was struck by her honest, deep-down warmth, effervescence, and drive. She also had the one quality that I look for above all others in an aspiring on-air talent: She was real! About a year or so later, Lisa's agent departed from our agency. At that point, Lisa's career was stagnant, so I met with her to see if there was a way we could jump-start her growth. Before doing so, I reviewed her demo reel (which we used to market her), and I realized that it was holding her back, as it showed her inexperience and didn't showcase the many gifts and wealth of knowledge that made her special. As a result, she lost out to more experienced and polished individuals with whom she was competing for on-air positions.

I listened intently to Lisa, and I was able to develop a strong sense of her wonderful value system, as well as the emotionally intelligent way that she viewed life. Most important, I learned that Lisa was an exceptional golfer and that she also had a good working knowledge of pro football. I then asked her what would "make her heart sing" professionally. She said that her *Goal* was to host reality-based television shows. With that information in hand, I began to develop our choreography. I told her that if her *Goal* was to have a career like that of Mary Hart, Nancy O'Dell, or Leeza Gibbons, she had to start doing live TV as soon as possible. The way to accomplish this, I explained, "is by leading with your strength, which, in this case, is focusing on your unique athletic background, both when we market you and when you interview." I told her that her athletic knowledge, when combined with her other talents, would set her apart from others, and, in some situations, would make up for her lack of on-air experience.

With this in mind, the next step was for me to call the general manager of KCBS, the Los Angeles CBS-owned station, which had an open position on their weekend sports program, *Sports Central*. This job called for someone to conduct a series of fun and lively interviews with fans after the pro-football game that KCBS had just finished airing. I knew that if Lisa could secure this position, it would be a great vehicle for her to develop her live television skills. It would also be a stellar showcase for her personality and love of sports. I would also contact the Golf Channel to see if they had any open positions that could take advantage of Lisa's unique golf expertise.

Based upon my enthusiastic recommendation, the KCBS general manager agreed to meet with Lisa the next day. Shortly after their meeting, he called to offer Lisa the Sunday "Fan-Cam" position.

We were on our way!

I then explained to Lisa that our Big-Picture Choreography wasn't to develop her as a sportscaster. It was to use her sports knowledge in order to gain on-air experience, and then, little by little, we would develop a much more polished and effective demo reel, which would enable her to transition into reality-based hosting.

Our choreography worked. After doing ten weekends of Fan-Cam interviews, Lisa received a call from Steve Tello, an executive at the Fox Sports Network. Steve's plan was to bring Lisa to Fox and groom her as a sportscaster. As Lisa needed a great deal more training and on-air experience, the Fox offer was a golden opportunity for her to grow and improve on an everyday basis. So the next steps were for her to accept the offer and make the most of the Fox position. Which she did.

Steve and the individuals at Fox were true to their word, as they worked hard to train Lisa and give her opportunities to shine. And Lisa, much to her credit, worked tirelessly to learn as much as she could.

After a year or so at Fox, the next step was for me to start sending out Lisa's new and dramatically improved demo reel to reality-show producers, which I did with great anticipation. Within weeks, Lisa was hosting a national, prime-time, reality-based show; thereafter, she hosted another. The strategy of "lead with your strength" helped Lisa fulfill her *Dream* of being a national host.

Strata-Gem

One very effective means of initiating a success-evoking choreography is to identify what your personal and professional strengths are, and to find a position that will use those strengths to your and your employer's best advantage . . . as you learn and grow.

THE
ENHANCING NICHE

One essential strategy for putting the percentages heavily in your favor that you will attain huge success is to identify your *Enhancing Niche*—a job, position, profession, or business that makes the most of your strengths, your skills, and your passions. You are much more likely to flourish if you're good at what you do and love doing it. So it is essential to understand what your personal gifts, skill sets, talents, and experiences are, as well as what your non-strengths and dislikes are. If you go through this process honestly and precisely, you will take a major step toward identifying the professions in which you will thrive.

For example, most National Football League quarterbacks will be more fruitful within one, specific form of offensive scheme than in another. Would Tom Brady, arguably the best quarterback ever, be as successful on a team that required him to throw the ball forty yards or more many times a game? Perhaps not. Bill Belichick, the New England Patriots' head coach, devised an offensive system that played to Brady's great strengths. In most instances, Brady's passes were about twenty yards or less, and only on occasion did he throw a pass of forty yards or more. This offensive plan worked with unprecedented success for Brady and the Patriots, as they played in nine Super Bowls together, winning six of them.

Decades ago, Oprah Winfrey was an anchor in Baltimore. From what I'm told, Oprah was a very good anchor, but not the megastar that she ultimately became as a host. In all likelihood, the reason why Oprah's gifts didn't shine as brightly as an anchor was that her newscasts were so tightly scripted and packed with "anchor reads" that she rarely had the opportunity to showcase her great ad-libbing and interviewing skills. But once Oprah became a morning-show host in Chicago, she quickly became one of the best hosts in the history of broadcasting—very possibly the best! Why the huge difference in success? Simply because one position didn't utilize Oprah's extraordinary strengths and unique skill set, while the other put them on full, radiant display.

Many consider Katie Couric to be the most successful female morning-show host ever. When interacting with and playing off the ensemble of *Today* show teammates, she and her gifts shone brightly. The fit was perfect! However, when she chose to leave the *Today* show to solo anchor the *CBS Evening News*, Katie's career trajectory took a dip. Why? Because as an anchor, she was reading to and talking at the viewers. Additionally, with no co-anchor, she had no one to banter with, have fun with, or play off of. This format did not take advantage of what makes Katie so watchable, special, and relatable. Plainly put, Katie agreeing to be a solo anchor and CBS News hiring her for that role appears to have been a disappointing move for all parties.

In hindsight, Katie could have learned from this experience and put the percentages of attaining future successes squarely in her favor by being a lead player in an ensemble, as she is a great chemistry facilitator and shines radiantly when paired with talented others. Perhaps Katie didn't recognize this reality when, for the next step in her career, she *solo*-hosted her own talk show. Unfortunately, Katie's show ended after its second season. One thing appears clear: Katie is truly extraordinary when she can interact on a regular basis with the right individuals; I hope that Katie's next big show incorporates this great gift.

Megyn Kelly was brilliant as the sharp-witted, occasionally controversial, and enormously engaging and compelling Fox News Channel anchor. She was killing it! But because she allegedly felt it was time to make a change, she decided to go to NBC and host the third hour of *Today*. Unfortunately, it appears that this move did not work out as Megyn and NBC initially envisioned it. From my vantage point, the main reason why the third hour of *Today* was not the right fit for Megyn was that she was rarely able to do the things that make her shine so brightly.

At Fox, Megyn thrived when discussing and conducting interviews on politics, hot-button issues, and major stories of the day. She was strong and incisive, and she held your attention. On the nine a.m. *Today* show, Megyn conducted far more show-appropriate lighter and softer interviews, which didn't play to or showcase her great harder-news strengths and what makes her so special. So the odds of her attaining the huge success that she enjoyed at Fox News were stacked against her. I very much look forward to the highly gifted Megyn hosting a program that showcases her tremendous talents.

Robin Meade, one of the best network morning-show hosts ever, has enjoyed a hugely successful run as the host of Headline News's (HLN's) *Morning Express with Robin Meade*. One of the main reasons why her audience is so loyal and why she and *Morning Express* are so popular is that the content, tone, feel, and segments of the show allow Robin to be truly authentic and they brilliantly showcase the gifts that make her so exceptional. *Morning Express* is the perfect success-evoking show for Robin.

As a skillful choreographer, you need to spend time carefully thinking about and identifying what jobs and positions will make the most of what you're good at, your education and experiences, and what you like or love to do. You want to accept and be in positions that take advantage of who you are, what makes you special, and who you aspire to be. By doing this, you put the percentages strongly in your favor that you will enjoy a highly successful and rewarding career experience.

Strata-Gem

It is essential to choose positions that showcase your gifts, skills, and knowledge. By doing this, you significantly increase the chances that you will be successful, appreciated, and happy.

14

DOES YOUR DISCONTENT
LIE WITH YOUR WORK
OR WITH YOUR JOB?

In counseling an unhappy or unfulfilled client, I often ask, "Are you dissatisfied with the work you're doing, or rather with the environment or the people you're working for or with?"

This is a key question. If you like what you're doing, but you're in an unsupportive or toxic environment, then your choreography must be to find a supportive and enhancing company or set of associates with whom you can do the same or similar work, and flourish. If, however, you don't derive any satisfaction or pleasure from what you do every day, then you must take the necessary time to construct your *Clarifying List* so you can identify and seek out work that will take advantage of your unique set of strengths, skills, experiences, needs, and passions.

The German philosopher Goethe once wrote: "If you treat an individual as he is, he will remain how he is. But if you treat him as if he were what he ought to be and could be, he will become what he ought to be and could be."[7] If you're in an unsupportive or negative environ-

---

7   Johann Wolfgang von Goethe, *Wilhelm Meister's Apprenticeship [Wilhelm Meisters Lehr-jahre]*, 1796.

ment, you are less likely to perform well and thrive than when you're in a supportive and nurturing one. I know that I've performed far better as a tennis player for coaches who believed in me and expected the best from me.

This was the case with my freshman coach at Harvard, Corey Wynn. During my competitive tennis career, I had more-accomplished coaches, but I never played better than I did for Corey. He thought that I was great, and he never expected me to lose—and I never lost for him. His belief in me inspired me and lifted my performances. Because I felt safe with him and supported by him, I was never afraid to take a risk on the court and push the envelope in order to improve and grow. How great and empowering is that?

This calls to mind the day pro tennis player Lindsay Davenport defeated Martina Hingis to win the 1998 U.S. Open Women's Singles title. In discussing her road to success, Davenport, during her post-victory CBS interview, reflected, "People have said I'm not the one that's gonna do it; I'm not the one that's gonna make it, and I've truly tried not to let that bother me, and really just tried to keep improving and stick to myself and stick to the people close around me that have really believed in me."[8]

In my over thirty-five years of career and life counseling, I have found that people are far more likely to reach their potential, do great things, work harder, and derive much more fulfillment when they work with and for individuals who are encouraging and constructive.

When you work, you are a *performer*, as you perform the functions that your position requires. In almost all instances, you will perform far better if you work for people who believe in and support you. Therefore, before you accept a job, it is critical to your

---

8   CBS Sports U.S. Open Final post-game interview, https://www.youtube.com /watch?v=4p3rDWrHaC8.

consistent and sustained success and happiness that you accurately assess the people you'll be working for. And, if you're currently working for or with individuals who are toxic, and the situation isn't remediable, then you must think seriously about choreographing a change.

It is also of great importance to work with people who believe in you. One of the advantages my clients have is that they are emotionally and intellectually buoyed by my strong belief in their potential for long-term success, even during their career hiccups and their most insecure times. Likewise, it is tremendously advantageous for you to associate and align yourself with positive and constructive individuals who see the best in you. It will make the trials and tribulations that you will inevitably go through during your career journey so much easier to weather. This belief and support can also contribute to your short-term and long-term success.

Strata-Gems

1. Your goal is to work with supportive, enhancing, and positive individuals.

2. You want to work in a field that you enjoy, that you find stimulating and challenging, and about which you are passionate.

3. Don't work for a jerk!

DESIRE

It's nice to say that you "aspire"
And that the Choreography you craft will take you higher,
But success isn't attained without the internal fire
Of the catalyzing emotions of want and desire!

So be passionate, present, and engaged
In whatever you pursue and do!

—K.L.

15

BE PASSIONATE ABOUT AND ENGAGED IN WHAT YOU DO

The harder I work, the luckier I get!

—SCOTT FREEDMAN, winner of the most
national POP Tennis/paddle tennis singles
and doubles titles in the history of the sport

We have already discussed how crucial it is to your success and happiness that your job, career, or profession incorporate things that you're good at, and that you work with supportive individuals. It is also vital to do something that you enjoy or are passionate about. Why? Because if you aspire to attain sustained success, in most instances, you've got to really want it and you have to be intensely focused on attaining it. If you lack either the requisite desire or focus, it will be too easy for you to be diverted into settling for more immediate and ultimately less-gratifying substitutes.

Desire is a powerful concept and force. It conjures up high-energy qualities such as passion, need, want, and the like. When these emotion-based energies are channeled toward healthy and constructive ends, they can have a huge, positive impact upon your *Goal*-attaining efforts. These energies can initially have a catalyzing effect on you. Thereafter, they can help you sustain your efforts and focus, as you face problems, crises, distractions, and weak moments.

At all costs, avoid hiding your true feelings from yourself to protect your ego in the event you don't succeed in your quest. To the contrary, you must clearly identify your *Goals*, and not be afraid to put yourself on the line in your efforts to achieve them. Being dialed in to your *Goal*-attainment journey, both internally and externally, will enable you to enjoy the process and the victories so much more.

For example, I vividly remember the semifinal match of the 2005 French Open tennis tournament. Nineteen-year-old newcomer Rafael Nadal was playing Roger Federer, the number-one player in the world for the previous three years. In prior matches, I had noticed how focused and passionate Nadal was as he defeated opponent after opponent. In this match, the same held true. On the first point, Federer had Nadal running from side to side; he then hit a rocket forehand that sent Nadal running across the court, only for Nadal to hit a spectacular running winner. That one extraordinary shot by Nadal, that burst of speed, that intense passion, set the tone for the rest of the match. By his actions, Nadal told Federer in the most explicit and emphatic way, "I'm here, amped, dialed in, and coming at you!"

Upon seeing Nadal streak across the court and not only return Federer's excellent shot but also hit it for an outright winner, the commentator explained, "Well, you can see that Nadal is dialed in right from the first point." A few moments later, when Nadal won the first two games convincingly and Federer looked lethargic, the commentator remarked, "Roger better get engaged in their match, or he's going to have real trouble."

Those words were prophetic. Nadal was resolute, and immersed in his job, right from the start, and Federer, the number-one-seeded player, never seemed to be involved. The result: Nadal upset Federer. In fact, he dominated him! As it turned out, this match set the tone for the many future Nadal/Federer matches.

Those who reach extraordinary career heights are passionate about what they do, as well as engaged in the process. So it makes sense that if you want to be great at what you do, whenever possible, you must do things that you truly like or even love. Your positive energies can fuel great results!

YOUR HARD, FOCUSED WORK IS ESSENTIAL TO YOUR SUCCESS

As we are discussing the virtues of being dialed in, focused upon, and passionate about giving your best professional efforts on a daily basis, it is crucial to reinforce how important having a strong work ethic can be in your *Goal*-attaining strategy.

Throughout my adult life, I have seen that it is often the person who works the hardest and the most strategically who enjoys the sweet fruits of success. Time and time again I have observed that great talent can be reduced to mere potential, unless it is combined with smart, hard work. That said, if you do successfully coalesce your talent with a strong work ethic, you put the percentages very much in your favor that you will be a Career Choreography rock star!

Strata-Gems

1. If you want to attain maximum success, you must be engaged in and diligent and passionate about what you do.

2. It will be easier to be fully engaged if you identify and pursue your passion(s).

3. If you aspire to enjoy great and sustained job or career success, your hard, smart work is essential.

GETTING IT RIGHT—FROM THE START

Getting it right, from the start,
Can certainly play a material part,
In giving you a solid crack,
At starting on the faster track.

It's true that you aren't assured of winning,
Just because you've had a good beginning.
But all too often, you will find,
You can't catch up, once you're behind.

Life is easier, I suspect,
If from the start, you've earned respect.
Having the right mindset, when you begin,
May well pay off with a coveted win.

In the working world, first impressions count,
So starting strong is paramount!

—K.L.

16

FAVORABLE FIRST IMPRESSIONS AND FULFILLING FINISHES

You can only make a first impression once!

—Unknown

First impressions and fast starts can and do play material roles in *Goal* attainment. Sam Weisbord, former president of the William Morris Agency, told me this enlightening and inspiring story about his early success. Sam began his William Morris career in the mail room delivering mail and packages, and performing other menial tasks. After about a year or so, he was assigned to fill in for a week for one of the two assistants to Abe Lastfogel, the chairman of the board.

During this short period, Mr. Lastfogel held a late-night, executives-only meeting. At 8:30 p.m., Mr. Lastfogel's regular assistant, Eric, left to go home, but Sam stayed. During the meeting, which lasted until after midnight, Sam sat outside Mr. Lastfogel's office and took copious shorthand notes, as Sam was able to hear everything that transpired because the office door was ajar. Two days later, a heated argument ensued between two executives as to what had actually been said by one of the executives at that late-night meeting. That's when Sam respectfully volunteered to read his letter-perfect transcription of the dialogue that had taken place during the meeting. After his notes had been read, the discrepancy was cleared up. Mr. Lastfogel was impressed, and the next morning Sam was promoted to executive assistant, leapfrogging over Mr. Lastfogel's other assistant, Eric, who had left the office hours earlier. Eric had been Mr. Lastfogel's top assistant for nearly two years.

Two clichés seem appropriate here as a means of reinforcing some of the points raised by this story:

1. Preparation (Sam mastering his shorthand note-taking skills and staying late to take copious notes) met opportunity (the need for dispute resolution), and Sam seized the moment. This resulted in his career being put on the fast track.

2. Regarding the longtime assistant, Eric, who chose not to stay in the office until the late-night meeting had concluded, I would say: "If you choose to snooze and just cruise—you set the stage to at some point lose!"

I cannot begin to recount the many instances that I've witnessed where an individual got off on the right foot, be it with an endeavor or in a relationship, and it paid off in major dividends. For Sam Weisbord, such a progression certainly took place, as he ultimately became the president of the William Morris Agency. However, first impressions and fast starts can only carry the day for so long. In Sam's case, the reason he was elected president by the board of directors is because of the *consistent* and *sustained* successes that he enjoyed during the decades that he worked for William Morris leading up to that fateful board of directors' vote.

Here's the key: In order for you to attain your full potential and enjoy consistent success over time, you must bring your A-game to the table every day. By doing this, not only will you increase the chances that you will get off to a favorable start, but just as important, you will enjoy fulfilling and rewarding journeys throughout your career, as well as brilliant and gratifying finishes!

On the other hand, many of the most successful individuals the world has known didn't get off to positive starts. This was the case with Michael Jordan, who allegedly failed to make his high-school basketball team. However, a lackluster beginning didn't hurt the evolution of a historically successful career. Jordan grew to become arguably the best basketball player ever. I'm told that Pete Sampras wasn't the top junior tennis player in the U.S., but he grew to be one of the very best tennis players in the history of the sport. No one thought that my dad had any professional potential, and he was fired from his first important job in America, yet he went on to have a legendary eighty-year off-price retailing career. These three superstars in their fields certainly proved all of their naysayers wrong! For these hugely successful individuals and for so many others, a poor first impression didn't preclude a fantastic and fulfilling finish.

Remember: Your Career Choreography isn't a sprint. It's a highly strategic marathon.

Strata-Gem

Making a good (or great) first impression can be tremendously advantageous in getting off to a fast start in a new relationship or endeavor. This is something to strive for. However, a good first impression is only *one* enhancing step in your *Goal*-Attainment Choreography. The key is to have sustained and consistent success. This is accomplished over time by consistently being the sharpest and best performer you can be. Each day, with each challenge, strive to be great at what you do. And even though greatness is rarely achieved, taking your game to the highest level possible will put the percentages in your favor that you will attain truly gratifying and successful outcomes.

LAY A ROCK-SOLID MINDSET AND SKILL-SET FOUNDATION

There is absolutely no substitute for
substance and knowing your craft.

—JACK LINDNER

There is a beautiful Italian word, "Sprezzatura," which, loose-
ly translated, means "Work hard and lay a strong foundation of
knowledge, honed instincts, and skills; then let the fruits of your
labors flow smoothly and shine brightly when you need them!"

—ROBERT MITCHELL AND KEN LINDNER

The means by which you become really good—and even great—at what you do, and attain success, is by insightfully choreographing and then taking the requisite steps to lay a solid foundation in your chosen field or area of pursuit. If you want to become a successful doctor, attorney, plumber, hair or makeup stylist, manufacturer, entrepreneur, or any kind of leader or executive, you must know your stuff! It is crystal clear that *there is absolutely no substitute for substance!* In our society, oftentimes style overshadows substance, and the end receives more positive attention than the means. However, at critical or pivotal moments—crunch times!—when true stars in their field rise and stand out, and unprepared paper dragons flame out, you want and need to be at your very best. You must know what to do, how to do it—or at least be able to figure these things out, oftentimes on the fly—and have the experience, poise, and ability to effectively implement your choreographies. To put the percentages squarely in your favor that you will consistently attain success and rise above challenges, you need a rock-solid foundation of knowledge, real-life experiences, and honed instincts and intuition upon which to rely and by which to be guided. If you do not have this solid foundation, you will fail to maintain consistent and sustained success.

Always remember that substance matters, and content counts!

You may recall my example of knowledge coming to the fore at the right time in my dad's case. As a mere receiving-room clerk, he was summoned by the president of his department-store chain after my dad had taken the initiative to order several hundred women's suits for the sportswear department. Because my dad knew his stuff thoroughly and could persuasively explain his observations and actions—which later proved to be spot-on and highly profitable— he not only wasn't fired but was rewarded with a big promotion.

Continually maintaining this solid foundation directly contributed to my dad's enjoyment of a rewarding and gratifying (nearly) thirty-year second career—beginning at age sixty-nine! In an industry that covets youth and what's new, it was because my dad had such a great knowledge base and set of skills, and trusted his instincts, that he remained a valuable and integral part of the T.J. Maxx operation until his retirement at age ninety-eight. This is a testament to what having the right foundation can do for you and your career's longevity.

Besides, when you truly know that you have the goods, you feel like a rock star. What an empowering place to be when you face any challenge or obstacle, or go into an important meeting!

Anyone who aspires to be a master of his or her craft, profession, business, or hobby must commit to continually learning from every experience and individual they encounter. The key is that you must be a hungry perpetual student and a discerning talent emulator.

Think of your foundation development as a bank account. Every experience you have, good or bad, and every observation you make, is a deposit into your account. The more you learn and grow, the richer in knowledge and wisdom you become. And the more effective you are at attaining and making the most of your wisdom and insights, the more successful you are likely to be. So, keep the currency coming!

This concept was vividly reinforced by Captain Chesley "Sully" Sullenberger when he was interviewed by my client, Dan Ashley, regarding Captain Sullenberger's heroic landing of a U.S. Airways plane in the Hudson River after both of the plane's engines failed. When Dan asked whether training or experience had enabled the captain to successfully navigate such an extremely difficult and dangerous challenge, Sullenberger responded:

> We train for one engine loss, not two . . . Training is not the same as [experiencing] something in real life.
>
> Every time you experience something, you add it to your bank of experience from which you can draw. All of my education; all of my training; all of my experiences ended up being a critical mass from which I could draw upon that day.[9]

---

9   Sullenberger, Captain "Sully," interview by Dan Ashley, Evening KGO Newscast, February 17, 2009, https://vimeo.com/465893073/fadf3bbb9c.

What you can glean from the heroic captain's words is this: The more you learn, the more you know, and the more real-life experiences you have, the more you're likely to intuit what the best course of action is to take in a given situation. All of this knowledge was stored in Sullenberger's intellectual and instinctual bank account because he was, throughout his forty-year career, an active and respectful student and account depositor. Captain Sullenberger's inspiring story is a great illustration of the concept of *sprezzatura*, mentioned earlier, as all of his hard work, knowledge, and honed instincts organically became available to him when he, his crew, and his passengers needed them most.

I've known many individuals who can do one or more things (naturally) well, but who don't spend the time or make the effort to develop other necessary skills so they have an all-around, impenetrable skill-set foundation. For example, this would be the case when a doctor is good at fixing a problem but is poor as a diagnostician or lacks people skills—that doctor is an incomplete professional. Or someone may have the skills to open up potential areas of business but doesn't have the knowledge, training, or confidence to advance the deal or close it. An all-too-common problem for professionals, such as attorneys, doctors, dentists, and the like, is that they can be wonderful practitioners, but their businesses go bankrupt because they're not astute businesspeople. I've witnessed many unsuccessful individuals who are great starters, but who have never taken the time or made the effort to develop the balanced and diverse skill-set foundation in order to stay the course and be a great finisher. I've seen a number of individuals who have excellent ideas and creative visions, but who lack the skills to effectively implement them so as to make them a successful reality. Developing a *complete foundation* gives you every opportunity to do it all! You don't want to be a fatally flawed one-trick pony, as your shortcomings will cause you to fail to fulfill your fullest potential.

Finally, when you have a solid foundation, you will produce your success by design—not by luck or an occasional fortuitous circumstance. Once again, no one-hit wonders for us! It's nice to be lucky and to have good things happen to you as a result, but you can't rely on good fortune to bring you consistent success.

Always remember, if you develop the right foundation, you can succeed for a lifetime! Or, as the Amir clothing ad says, "Fashion is fleeting; style is forever!" So, have style, and know all that is necessary to bring you sustained success.

Strata-Gems

1. An invaluable component of achieving success is developing a rock-solid, reliable mindset and skill-set foundation.

2. Continue throughout your career to be a student of your craft by assimilating and analyzing data.

3. A stroke of luck can be beneficial, but if you desire to attain consistent and sustained success, you must produce it yourself by having the requisite intellectual, emotional, and (if necessary) physical goods.

4. Hope or luck is not the basis for consistent success.

SECURE THE MOST BENEFICIAL TRAINING EXPERIENCES

One of the primary means of developing the solid foundation we've discussed is to proactively seek out the most appropriate and effective training experiences possible. The way to accomplish this is to honestly identify what you don't know and what skills you need—or haven't yet mastered—and then find the best venues for equipping yourself with these tools. For example, if you require more schooling, learn whether a theoretical, a practical, or a mixture of both approaches will be the most beneficial means for you to achieve your *Goals* and *Dreams*. If, on the other hand, you believe that on-the-job training will be your best teaching vehicle, then you must decide whether you have the requisite knowledge or the necessary experiences to flourish in a nonstructured environment where you're expected to know your stuff without the help of anyone assigned to teach or mentor you. Or do you opt to start more slowly within the structured environment of a company that understands you're still learning, and therefore provides instruction and guidance along the way?

When explaining these concepts to my clients, I ask them to picture an ice-skating boot. Generally, it's made of soft leather, which provides little support and structure for a weak ankle or in the event of a false move. On the other hand, a rollerblading boot is strong and keeps your foot firmly in place, so there is little chance of turning an ankle, even if you are inexperienced or your ankle is weak. It provides great support.

If you already have enough experience, then getting started in an unstructured environment may be your best alternative. But if you're just starting out or not yet ready to be thrown into a demanding or potentially career-decimating sink-or-swim situation, then beginning slowly and surely, with appropriate support, may be the wise way to go.

Remember, if you start out slowly, the worst that can happen is that you're a big fish in a pond with less-experienced fish. You'll look great! But at least you won't drown in a pond that you weren't ready for. Generally, your best choreography bet is to start out in a structured rollerblading-boot environment. Then, when you're ready, go for the looser, unstructured ice-skating-boot experience.

Strata-Gems

1. In developing the strongest and most diverse work/career foundation possible, it is important to know what you need to learn and what skills you need to master.

2. In choosing the most beneficial on-the-job training venue for your development, decide how much structure and supervision you require so you can derive the most from the experience and perform at your best.

STARTING YOUR CAREER WITH AN ESTABLISHED, REPUTABLE COMPANY

A few months ago, "Austin" and I met at the suggestion of his parents, who are close friends of our family. Austin, who is twenty-six, is smart, has great people skills, and has a striking appearance. After exploring a number of fields, he decided to pursue becoming a real estate broker in the high-end, single-home arena. His questions for me were focused on how he might choreograph his real estate career, with his main question being whether he should initially work for an established firm to get his career going.

I explained to Austin that learning at a firm with individuals who are experts in his field of interest was an excellent idea. The wide-ranging knowledge he could gain, the varied experiences he would have, the different styles of selling he would be exposed to, and the invaluable contacts he could make are all huge benefits of working for a big, reputable firm. After spending a few years there, he could then decide whether he would want to stay and grow at that firm, go to another, or go off on his own. By getting all of this under his belt at a big firm, he would have the foundation to be successful no matter what path he eventually takes. I then told him that starting out and getting a terrific education at an established firm would be similar to my choreography of starting my career at the prestigious William Morris Agency, and years later choosing to open up my own agency. Looking back, I unquestionably received an excellent education and made many valuable contacts at William Morris.

Throughout the years, I have often counseled young adults to learn and grow at established firms in their chosen field as a highly efficacious means to lay a strong foundation for future career successes. For many, it's a perfect early step in their Career Choreography.

Strata-Gem

When beginning a career or making a career change, your best first step may be to work for an established, reputable firm or company. This way, you will receive excellent training and make important contacts.

HUNGER, COMPLACENCY, AND PREPARATION

You don't make the club (sitting) in the hot tub!

—UNKNOWN

Yesterday is history; tomorrow is a mystery.
Today is a gift, which is why they call it "the present."

—MIKE DITKA, NFL Hall of Fame member
and football commentator

A dean of a prominent Ivy League university recently confided to me that his school's alumni—both undergrads and graduate students—weren't succeeding out in the working world, the reason being: "Now that they have their degrees, they think that everything's coming to them. There's a strong and pervasive sense of entitlement out there. They feel like all they have to do is show up and that's enough! It's very troubling."

I agree with this observation. I have encountered way too many individuals in our society—especially relatively young ones—who expect to be successful without putting the necessary time, energy, thought, passion, analysis, and discipline into their jobs and careers. Talent, education, looks, and charisma will only get you so far! You must combine these gifts with your focused, insightful, conscientious commitment and hard work.

Almost everything in life—if it is worth attaining—involves competition. And if you aren't focused, committed, and passionate about succeeding, and if you phone it in or expect that it's all simply coming to you, someone with equal or more talent—who wants it more than you do[10]—may well be the one who enjoys the successful outcome. And, if that other individual is passionate, engaged, and enjoying the pursuit process—and you're not—in all likelihood, he or she will also be more successful than you at experiencing a fulfilling journey.

You want to be successful? Then always remember this: If you coast—you're toast!

One more misperception: "All you have to do is show up (and you'll find success)." Let's be clear. If you don't "show up" when the choreography calls for it, in all likelihood, you will have NO chance of being successful in your endeavor. However, just showing up does not in any way lead to consistent or sustained success in and of itself. "Showing up"—or not being afraid to put yourself on the line at the risk of failure—is, most times, simply one step in a *Goal-Attainment Choreography*. It is rarely the only step.

---

10   Please recall the story of Sam Weisbord, who was filling in for the chairman of the board's assistant. Sam stayed late to take copious notes of a meeting while the other permanent assistant went home. Sam's notes were thereafter needed for the resolution of a dispute. As a direct result of Sam's being "Johnny-on-the-Spot," he was promoted to the position of the chairman of the board's number-one assistant, taking the other assistant's place in the hierarchy.

Strata-Gem

Consistent, sustained success won't come to you simply because you expect it, because you perceive that you're entitled to it, or just by your showing up. True sustained and consistent success requires real, focused, thoughtful, and effective choreographed efforts—made over time.

THE DIFFICULTY OF MAINTAINING OR INCREASING SUCCESS

Never let your name, reputation, or position be greater
than your production. Celebrate rarely; grind daily.

—COLIN COWHERD

In any field, it's one thing to reach a level of success, stature, and credibility, but it's quite another thing to stay there.

In any given sport, for example, when you're the top seed or the favorite in some competition, everyone is gunning to take what you've attained away from you. It's a law of any jungle: If it's worth attaining, others will want it, and so you must work hard (and be smart) in order to keep it. In Chapter 15, we discussed Rafael Nadal's upset victory over Roger Federer the day before Nadal won the finals of the French Open. Nadal and his bright future were the talk of the sports world. But a mere two days later, Nadal lost in the first round of his next tournament to a virtual unknown. Such is the reality of the competitive professional jungle.

You can't rest on your laurels or be lulled into a state of self-satisfied complacency simply because you've experienced success. If you are to enjoy consistent and sustained success, you must remain hungry, sharp, and ahead of the curve. Believing your own press clippings, being fat and happy, not paying attention to detail, and forgetting the steps, strategies, focus, and tenacity that got you to where you are today are all recipes for slippage and setbacks. We live in an ultra-competitive, what-have-you-done-for-me-lately society. For you to enjoy ongoing success, you must stay on top of your game—at all times.

Once again, if you ride the wave of success too long without putting in the necessary effective effort, at some point, you're cruisin' for a success-diminution bruisin'. In the Choreography of Success, there are very few prolonged or sustained free rides. A rule of thumb: If you ride, you glide; or, you hide—you'll slide!

I learned this years ago as an athlete. Let me cite two examples for you. First, in college, I was playing in a prestigious men's open tennis tournament. I was to play Rod, a highly ranked, top-seeded player, in the quarterfinals. The day before our match, I watched Rod play. I noticed that his footwork was sloppy, and as a result, his shots weren't hit with the precision that I expected of a player of his caliber. He got away with a lackluster effort against his weaker opponent, but I believed that I had the skills to run Rod around and take advantage of his poor footwork, where his prior opponent didn't. What I also learned was that Rod earned his living as a tennis-teaching professional. As a result, he had been on the court giving lessons all day before he played his tournament matches. That's why he seemed so lethargic in his matches.

I, on the other hand, practiced and rested before I played Rod— and I beat him relatively easily: 6–2, 6–2. However, I was wise enough to know that if Rod hadn't been teaching all day prior to our match—but instead had been practicing and then resting as I had done—he would have played far better and might have beaten me. (I believed this because Rod, when he was on "the tour" just a few years earlier, had defeated some of the world's top players.)

I was later told that despite his teaching all day, Rod thought he would win our match "on reputation." The defining difference was that he didn't take the same preparatory steps to put himself in a position to win on a consistent and sustained basis as he had years earlier during his heyday. As a result, he now suffered many more defeats and far fewer gratifying victories. Essentially, as his commitment to keeping his skill set sharp decreased, the number of instances in which he enjoyed consistent success (according to his prior standards) precipitously decreased, as did his overall confidence!

Rod had abandoned the choreography that had initially brought him sustained success when he was a world-class player. As you seek to attain success, one paramount strategy for you to employ is this: Always be prepared; never forget the steps and strategies that initially advanced you; and take and implement those steps and strategies for as long as they remain potent.

During my senior year in college, I had the opportunity to play Arthur Ashe, who at the time was the fifth-ranked men's tennis player in the world, in an exhibition tennis match in my hometown of Brooklyn, New York. I had seen Arthur play numerous times, but he had never seen me play. As I watched his matches, I took notes detailing his shot-selection preferences. I practiced hours a day prior to the match on the very court on which we were to play. I had every advantage going for me, and I was mentally, physically, and technically prepared to play at the top of my game. Which I did, as I defeated him on that occasion. The next year, Arthur was ranked number one in the world and we were to play again. Only this time, I had a tennis-instruction business and was on the courts either teaching or managing many hours each day. As the day of the match grew closer, I began to get into better shape, but not good-enough shape. I began to practice with more intensity—but practicing was by no means as good a preparation as the highly competitive college and tournament schedule that had fine-tuned me prior to my playing Arthur the year before. Long story short, Arthur beat me easily and decisively. As we walked off the court at the conclusion of our match, the always-gracious Arthur said, "I was ready for you this time. But what happened to *you*?"

What happened to me was exactly what had happened to Rod, whom I discussed in the first story:

1. I forgot how important it was to be prepared, focused, tenacious, and passionate about my craft.

2. I didn't follow the tried-and-true success-evoking preparation choreography that had enabled me to reap many sweet tennis successes—including my defeat of Arthur the year before—throughout my playing career.

Always remember: *Effective preparation is an essential element of success!* Two more points are important to raise here:

1. Becoming successful and staying successful frequently require similar steps; however, often it requires even *more* passion, hunger, and focus to *remain* on top or stay successful over time because others want what you have, and you and what you have attained have become open targets. Just because you've attained some level of success doesn't necessarily mean it's going to be easy or easier to either maintain your success or enhance it—just ask any defending champion in any sport how hard it was to repeat his or her success.

2. I am not making any kind of value judgment here, such as "You must keep climbing the success-ladder in order to be deemed 'successful.'" As we will discuss in the final chapter of this book, success is a subjective and purely personal concept and benchmark. But, if you're going to continue to compete and attempt to secure your *Goals* and *Dream(s)*, stay sharp, proactive, and hungry, and keep improving and evolving.

Strata-Gems

1. If you desire to maintain or increase your success, you must maintain and possibly ratchet up your passion, focus, proactivity, and effectiveness.

2. If you want to attain consistent success, you must consistently engage in effective preparation and continue to evolve.

THE IMPORTANCE OF DISCIPLINE AND DELAYED GRATIFICATION

*By practicing the art of discipline at the appropriate times,
you can accomplish great and supremely gratifying things.
Without discipline, you won't consistently accomplish
anything truly worthwhile. It's your choice!*

—K.L.

Throughout my career, I've counseled that no strategies are more essential for achieving your *Goals* and *Dreams* than being disciplined and delaying gratification at the appropriate times and in the appropriate instances.

The other day, I saw a catchy advertisement for an ice-cream company; the tagline essentially read, "Life's uncertain—so what the heck, have the dessert *now*!" Life *can* be uncertain, but that doesn't mean you have a free pass to do away with delaying gratification if and when there is a more valuable, sought-after, and self-enhancing *Goal*—such as staying on your diet in order to lose weight or to keep your cholesterol or diabetes under control—that can be achieved with appropriate discipline.

Our quick-fix, I-want-it-all-now society constantly reinforces the benefits of going for immediate gratification. But oftentimes, opting for immediate gratification is like settling for the brass ring instead of striving for the gold—it is counterproductive and may well negate your long-term big-picture success. Achievers have learned how to distinguish between the situations when it is appropriate to go for the immediate gratification—while not sustaining any real long-term loss or damage—and when they must be disciplined enough to take the more difficult, less sexy or alluring, and more tedious road, so as to put them in the best position to receive a much more gratifying, fulfilling, and soul-nourishing payoff later.

Individuals who achieve their most cherished *Goals* and *Dreams* know that incorporating appropriate discipline in both their choreography construction and its implementation is crucial to achieving success. In the case studies cited earlier, the use of delayed gratification by Nancy O'Dell and my dad were integral steps in the attainment of their *Dreams*. For example—

1. Nancy O'Dell had the alluring opportunity to make a meteoric rise from being a local TV anchor in Charleston, South Carolina, to becoming a national host on the E! entertainment network. However, she knew she had more skills to polish before making such a move, so she instead chose to forgo the immediate gratification of accepting the alluring E! position. As a result, several years later, she secured a far more prestigious, far more lucrative, and far better position for her—that of *Entertainment Tonight* co-host, which was her *Dream*!

2. Even though my dad didn't realistically expect that he would one day have a second long-term career after the age

of sixty-six, he remained disciplined about his exercise regimen and his diet, he continued to maintain his work-related contacts, and he always stayed informed. He consciously *chose* to delay the short-term gratification of letting himself go, physically and intellectually, during his retirement. He chose not to eat fattening foods and gain weight. He chose not to fall out of touch with valuable contacts and lose track of what was new and "happening" in the industry that he dreamed about someday returning to in a meaningful, long-term way. Practicing appropriate discipline put him in the extraordinary position to enjoy a legendary second career . . . until he was ninety-eight.

Years ago, Lester Holt and I were having a conversation about his vacation plans. At the time, Lester was the host of *Dateline NBC*, the co-host of *Weekend Today*, and the anchor of the network's weekend *Nightly News*. He told me that Brian Williams, the anchor of NBC's Nightly *News*, needed to take four weeks off to undergo knee-replacement surgery. As a result, Lester was assigned to fill in for Brian for three weeks as the anchor of *NBC Nightly News*. Immediately thereafter, Lester and his wife, Carol, were to go on a long-awaited trip to Scotland.

However, at the time, ABC *World News Tonight* was moving up in the TV ratings and was dangerously close to overtaking *Nightly News* as the broadcast-news leader. As a result, the new president of NBC News, Deborah Turness, asked Lester if he could postpone his trip so that he could fill in for Brian for one additional week, with the goal of helping *Nightly* maintain its ratings position. Although Lester and Carol were eagerly anticipating their trip abroad, Lester recognized that this was an instance in which he needed to delay gratification and stay and fill in for the additional week—especially since his new division head made it a personal request.

As it turned out, Lester's decision to practice the art of delayed gratification served him extremely well, as he shone brightly in this fill-in role; NBC News maintained its ratings lead over ABC News; and the new head of the news division was deeply grateful that Lester postponed his vacation and helped NBC win the ratings competition that week. A couple of years later, when Brian was removed as the anchor of *Nightly News*, Lester was the natural choice to replace him, in large part because the ratings were so strong when Lester had filled in for Brian.

When it comes to exercising discipline, one of the main questions you must ask yourself is whether forgoing the immediate gratification may substantially increase your chances of attaining your *Goals* and *Dreams*. If going for the immediate gratification may damage your *future opportunities*, then you need to resist the glittering prize before you and think long term—however attractive the prize may seem. A constructive rule of thumb is this: You don't want to do anything that might conflict with or alter a path that may well lead you to attain your heart's truest desires.

No choreography catastrophes or casualties for you!

DIANA'S DISCIPLINED CHOREOGRAPHY

Here's another illustration of how being disciplined enough to delay gratification at the right time paid off with huge career dividends for "Diana," one of my clients.

Diana worked at a major advertising agency. Her immediate boss, "Alanna," was a senior account executive. Diana was young, hungry, smart, and talented. She loved what she did, and her *Dream* was to become a senior partner at her firm. Alanna was relatively young as well but was no longer as hungry as she once was. Certain company senior executives felt that over the past two years or so,

Alanna had been resting on her laurels and had become a bit full of herself. These execs began to begrudge and rethink the high salary that Alanna was being paid, but not necessarily earning.

Then, one day, Alanna was assigned an important and prestigious ad campaign that needed her and her staff's immediate attention. She was also told that Diana would work directly with and for her on this project. However, the timing of this assignment couldn't have been worse for the two of them. Alanna had scheduled a sixteen-day trip to Europe with her husband, starting the following week, and Diana was to be married in three days and immediately thereafter take a nine-day honeymoon.

Diana called me to strategize. She heard through the grapevine that Alanna was going to take her trip as scheduled—despite the company's and the client's pressing needs. Diana also wanted to take her honeymoon as scheduled, but she knew this would be a golden opportunity for her in many ways—and that it was appropriate and wise to be there for her company and its clients when they truly needed her.

My advice was for her to postpone her honeymoon—as long as it didn't cause a major problem with her fiancé. And, if she was able to do this, she should make sure that the execs in her company knew that she had done this for them. Diana's husband-to-be agreed that this was crunch time! It was a defining moment in which Diana could show her stuff—especially if Alanna took her trip as originally planned.

As it turned out, Alanna did take her trip, much to the consternation of her bosses. (Talk about hammering a bunch of nails into the coffin of failure!)

Diana, on the other hand, took center stage by staying, seized the moment, and wowed everyone. From that point on, Diana's career was immeasurably enhanced and placed firmly on a faster and more visible track. Three months later, Alanna was told that she had a month to look for other employment. Upon Alanna's departure, Diana was promoted to Alanna's position.

This is just one of an abundance of examples I can cite in which being disciplined, coming up *big* at the appropriate time, and keeping your *Goals* and *Dreams* at the fore and in crystal-clear focus have absolutely enabled the choreographers to achieve their most positive potential and cherished *Goals*.

I cannot stress enough how very center-stage the strategy of using appropriate discipline should be in your *Goal*-attaining efforts. With discipline, you can accomplish great and supremely gratifying things. Without discipline, you won't consistently accomplish anything truly worthwhile. It's your choice.

Strata-Gem

Appropriate use of discipline and its soulmate, delayed gratification, is an invaluable success-attaining strategy.

CONSTRUCTIVELY SLOG THROUGH TEDIOUS AND DIFFICULT ASSIGNMENTS

There are some, or even many, unenjoyable things that you need to do, so that you can do the things that you most want to do.

—JACK LINDNER

When it comes to "slogging"— constructively do it and just get through it!

—K.L.

On one hand, a major key to experiencing both success and happiness is to do what makes your heart sing! However, all high achievers know that along with doing and achieving what makes your heart sing, you must also do things that aren't enjoyable or challenging. In fact, these tasks may be dreadfully boring and painstaking. But these necessary evils will ultimately prepare and equip you to achieve some bigger and more fulfilling *Goals* and *Dreams*.

For example, athletes must train and practice so that they put themselves in the best position to win when they compete. Doctors must go through years of extensive training in order to be practice-ready. Most individuals who begin their careers at a talent agency must start in the mail room and perform endless, mindless tasks. Hair colorists are usually assistants first. Essentially, anyone who wants to succeed must do their homework and training, perform tedious tasks, and have experiences that no one looks forward to. Such diligence is all part of laying the required foundation and taking the necessary steps in order to be successful.

I will always remember what the late NBA commissioner David Stern said after he received criticism in some circles for not allowing a trade of the New Orleans Hornets' star player, Chris Paul, to the Los Angeles Lakers—a trade that appeared to many to benefit all parties: "I knew we were doing the best thing for New Orleans and that was my job," Stern said. "You have to stick with what you think was right. I must confess it wasn't a lot of fun, but I don't get paid to have fun."[11]

Years ago, my dad explained, "There are some or many unenjoyable things that you need to do, so that you can do the things that you most want to do. You can either choose to have a good attitude and make it a positive experience for you and those you come into contact with, or you can make it a negative and poisonous one—which doesn't ever benefit you. Always remember that you can see, learn, and be far more alert and effective with your head, spirits, and antennae up, than when you're not at the ready or engaged—because you're brooding."

Successful individuals have accepted the reality that they often

---

11   Associated Press, *The Inquirer*, December 15, 2011, https://sports.inquirer.net/29127/hornets-clippers-agree-on-chris-paul-trade.

must slog through some or many boring, tedious, or distasteful tasks, assignments, or responsibilities along the way. The key is for you to be psychologically and emotionally adaptable. You want to slog in a constructive manner so that you put yourself through as little psychological pain as possible, as well as put yourself in the best position to achieve your *Goals* and *Dreams*.

Slogging is something that every successful individual does—sometimes, many times a day. Just do it and get through it in the most positive way possible. Learn from the experience, if possible, and remind yourself that you are slogging because doing so is a necessary step that may well enable you to one day do something greatly fulfilling and satisfying. And if you can do your best to enjoy, or at least not mind, the slogging, then all the better!

I have found that if you can dispense with the most boring or distasteful tasks first or early in your day and get them out of the way, you thereby free up the remainder of your day and your psyche for more fun and fulfilling tasks and endeavors. It's my "Worst-First Rule."

Strata-Gem

On the road to—and as a prerequisite of—attaining success, we all must do things we don't enjoy or even find truly unsatisfying, brainless, and/or distasteful. I refer to this unpleasant activity as *slogging*. If you want to achieve your *Goals* and *Dreams*, some or a good deal of slogging will be necessary. So just do it and get through it! It's an integral part of the Choreography of Success.

24

KNOW THE EXPECTATIONS OF YOUR EMPLOYERS, ASSOCIATES, AND CLIENTS

The value of knowledge is in its [effective] use.

—**LIMOR DANKNER**, Milken Community Schools
junior-high principal

One of the strategies I continually share with my clients is, if you want to maximize your potential to be successful, you must know or correctly intuit the expectations of others, such as your employers, associates, and clients or potential clients. This is because you're not functioning in a vacuum.

So many relationships go south and sour because the parties involved don't communicate, they miscommunicate, and/or they don't meet each other's expectations. Conversely, if you meet or exceed others' expectations, you put the percentages squarely in your favor that you will have a positive experience and outcome with whomever you interact. This accomplishment can be a major building block of your success and job enjoyment.

Years ago, an exceedingly talented and bright newscaster, "Kathy," joined a San Francisco TV station as an evening anchor. About two months into Kathy's stay there, without conferring with anyone, she unilaterally decided to travel to Los Angeles to purchase a new on-air wardrobe and get a new hairstyle because she perceived that her current assortment of clothes and hairstyle didn't fit the more conservative market that she was now in. After three days of wearing her new on-air attire, I got an irate call from her nearly frothing-at-the-mouth boss, telling me how much he hated Kathy's new outfits and hairstyle and that I should get her to stop wearing the "old lady clothes, today!" He abruptly ended our call by explaining that he had hired a stylish thirty-five-year-old young lady, "not Angela Lansbury!"

When I called Kathy to delicately broach the fact that her general manager didn't at all like her new clothes and hairstyle, she shot back that she had done her research, had gone to the best hairstylist in Los Angeles, and had spent a boatload of money on her new clothes. In exasperation, she ended by saying that the general manager "just doesn't appreciate me or anything I do!"

I let a few moments pass before I counseled Kathy: "*Before* you get your hair styled and go clothes shopping next time, have a conversation with your general manager. Ask him what *he* wants, because *he's* the one you're trying to please. Think of it this way—if you bring him the best sushi in town, but he hates sushi, you probably won't secure the desired positive response. However, if you know what he likes and what will make him happy, and you base your decisions on those preferences, you will greatly increase the chances that your actions will be received in a positive way."

From then on, Kathy got to know her general manager better so that she could correctly intuit what would please him. And when she wasn't relatively sure what he desired, she'd ask him. As a direct result, they developed a much stronger relationship—based upon knowledge and fulfilled expectations.

Strata-Gems

1. Your success and enjoyment in connection with an interaction or an endeavor can hinge upon whether or not you meet a key other's expectations, and whether or not that key other perceives and feels that you are both on the same page.

2. Some ways to know how to meet others' expectations are by (a) asking the key person what he or she wants and expects out of an interaction and then effectively listening to his or her responses; (b) asking other trustworthy and knowledgeable individuals (before the encounter in question) what that key person wants and expects; and (c) correctly intuiting, through observation and/or honed instincts, what that key person wants and expects.

3. Having the knowledge and the ability to meet others' expectations can create exceedingly positive interactions and strong relationships. It can also equip you to act and speak with great effectiveness.

25

SET YOURSELF APART
FROM YOUR COMPETITORS

One success-evoking strategy that a number of my clients have implemented is to create or adopt a means to stand out from and rise above the crowd.

For example, my client Lester Holt assumed the highly prestigious position of anchor of NBC's *Nightly News*. Unlike other anchors who appear to be tethered to their anchor chairs and desks, Lester takes full advantage of his excellent reportorial skills by personally covering important and impactful stories. Instead of merely reading stories about world events as other anchors do, Lester consciously decided to take his newscast *to* the story, frequently reporting on it firsthand.

By having a novel format that showcases his excellent reporting skills, Lester continues to add great value to his newscast, to NBC News, and to his career. All huge dividends and values added!

Another example of how Lester strategically sets his newscast apart from the pack are the heart-touching and soul-warming everyday hero stories that he and his *Nightly News* colleagues do to close the newscast most nights. Lester correctly perceives that with cable news and the Internet supplying us with moment-by-moment news updates, there are very few stories that people are not aware of by the time the network evening newscasts air. So it has been Lester's and his colleagues' goal to report the stories of the day better and with more relevance than do the other news outlets. *Nightly*'s everyday hero stories showcase Lester's authenticity, his credibility, and his genuinely beautiful soul. As a direct result, Lester is beloved and has become, by many people's standards, "the most trusted person in news." All of these well-conceived ideas positively separate Lester and *Nightly News* from the competition.

Oprah Winfrey is an excellent example of someone who was able, with unprecedented success, to break through the clutter of the then-existing set of daytime TV talk shows and become a megastar, as well as a hugely impactful influence and force in American culture. Somehow Oprah and her producers intuited what daytime viewers wanted or would gravitate to in a talk show. They correctly identified and created new talk-show segments and topics that were delivered in Oprah's unique way, and they struck viewer gold. As a direct result, the *Oprah Winfrey Show* became a humongous hit and daytime staple, and Oprah grew to be one of this country's most successful entrepreneurs and richest individuals. She is truly bigger than life! All of this has happened because Oprah was able to set herself and her show apart from the competition in an enhancing way.

Strata-Gem

A highly effective career strategy is to find creative ways for you and what you do to shine, and thereby positively set yourself apart from your competition.

COMPARTMENTALIZATION

During a recent flight to Miami, I was taken with how warm, friendly, and accommodating to everyone one of the flight attendants was. Toward the end of our flight, I complimented her on the way that her upbeat demeanor had made the flight more enjoyable for all of us. Upon receiving my compliment, she said that I had made her day, as she was having a "hellacious morning," especially because she was a single mom and had no choice but to leave her very sick young daughter at home with "some new sitter." Not only was she stressed out with too many things to do, but she felt terrible guilt about leaving her child with someone she didn't know.

What a thorough professional this woman was. She was able to separate or compartmentalize her feelings and her personal concerns so she could perform her job with great effectiveness. Pretty darn impressive!

NBA star Kobe Bryant was able to accomplish the same thing. After spending the entire day in a Colorado courtroom when he was in the thick of his Eagle, Colorado, trial, he raced back to Los Angeles late that afternoon to play—and star—that evening in a game that his Lakers team won. I was at that game, and no matter how you felt about Kobe's guilt or innocence or his debatable lack of morality regarding his alleged rape accusation, everyone was astounded as to how someone with such overwhelming outside pressures and distractions could perform so well on the court. What Kobe was able to do, with off-the-charts effectiveness, was to leave his pressing problems at the door and focus on being the best professional he was capable of, when he needed to do so.

Here is a personal story illustrating how important it was for me to compartmentalize my feelings and concerns. When I was a senior in college, my partner and I reached the finals of the biggest collegiate doubles tennis tournament that I would compete in. We were to play the number-one team from the University of Georgia, one of the top doubles teams in the country. That night, I continually called my tennis coach, but no one was home. Finally, at about midnight, when no one answered, I reasoned, "I have no idea where my coach is. He knows I am playing in a monumentally important tournament, and I haven't heard anything from him—even after leaving a couple of messages. Is he hurt? Is something wrong? Or maybe nothing is wrong. Who knows? But I've worked my whole college career to have the opportunity to win this tournament. Since worrying isn't going to do anything other than make me tired for tomorrow's match and divert my focus away from the major task at hand, I'm going to go to sleep, get my rest, keep my focus, and go out tomorrow and win the tournament." Which my partner, John Ingard, and I did: 7–6, 6–7, 7–6.

Early the next day, I heard from my coach. As it turned out, there was an attempted robbery at his home, and he was at the police station, and then at a hotel all night. When I heard what happened, I was proud of myself for not letting my angst from the night before the tournament finals distract me from giving my all the following day, and because the match was decided by just a couple of hotly contested points in the final-set tie-breaker, I needed all of the focused attention I could muster in order for us to win.

The strategy here is to not let events or situations over which you have no control distract you and diminish your focus, performance, or professionalism.

One way to put the percentages heavily in your favor that you will be successful in any professional or job-related endeavor is to separate or compartmentalize how you're feeling and what you are going through personally, and to leave all of it out of your professional life. Additionally, do not let the angst, frustration, and other negative feelings caused by other professional or job-related situations distract you from giving your all to the situation or to the client at hand.

When I was growing up, my dad always counseled me to "develop a personality that fits your business and one that will cause people to want to do business with you." You can only successfully accomplish this if your personal and/or professional challenges don't impede or preclude you from being someone with whom people want to work.

Strata-Gem

Everyone has personal problems and stress that must be dealt with. However, you must find a way to separate yourself from your distractions and leave them out of the professional dealings or interactions at hand.

RECOGNIZE DEFINING MOMENTS AND BE OPPORTUNISTIC

I came up small.

—CURT SCHILLING, star Major League Baseball player,
discussing a less-than-stellar performance at an important time

It's your goal to come up BIG when it counts the most.

—K.L.

All individuals, all assignments, all opportunities, and all accomplishments are not the same! Some are monumentally more important than others and have a great deal more to do with whether or not you attain your *Goals* and *Dreams*.

For example, Jennifer Jahanbigloo ("Jennifer J."), who is my friend "Brittany's" hair colorist, is great at what she does, and Brittany recommends her to everyone. These kinds of high-praise reviews have helped Jennifer build a very successful hair-color business and hair salon.

I was told that one day, Jennifer was unexpectedly given the golden opportunity to color Julia Roberts's hair on the set of Ms. Roberts's new film. The challenge was that Jennifer needed to be in Texas the very next morning, where Ms. Roberts was shooting. However, Jennifer's salon was in Beverly Hills, and she had a full slate of customers whose hair she was scheduled to color the following day.

Understanding that this was an opportunity that doesn't come along very often, if ever, Jennifer rescheduled the following day's appointments for later in the week or had her other colorists fill in for her. She then flew to Texas. Ms. Roberts apparently loved Jennifer's work, as she has since requested that Jennifer color her hair for other films. Implementing the strategy of zestfully and creatively seizing a major career-enhancing opportunity is what makes some individuals brilliant choreographers and highly successful.

As a result of this visible success, other motion-picture stars have requested Jennifer to color their hair. These successes, in turn, led Jennifer to accept a lucrative spokesperson position for a major hair-product company. Per the terms of the agreement, Jennifer received major advertising promotion as the hair colorist to major film stars—publicity that has been worth its weight in gold. Jennifer then developed her own hair-color line. Because of the positive exposure she received and the major company connections she developed, at least two top hair-care companies were interested in manufacturing and distributing Jennifer's products.

Success does breed success! But the success track that Jennifer is now on would far less likely have existed if she hadn't recognized that rearranging her schedule so she could fly to Texas the next day to color Julia Roberts's hair—and do a wonderful job—was a career-building, defining moment, which she absolutely had to seize!

Here's a similar story. A litigation attorney whom I know worked on various cases for his law firm. And during the first five years at this law firm, he did a fine job but hadn't accomplished anything that distinguished him from anyone else.

Then one day, he was exposed to a set of wrongful-death cases that smacked of an egregious wrong being perpetrated by very large companies against many thousands of individuals. (This situation resembles the one portrayed years ago in the film *Erin Brockovich*.) For the next year or so, that attorney—to the exclusion of almost everything else—immersed himself in researching and conducting interviews for what would become a huge class-action suit.

Two and a half years later, this attorney won a precedent-setting award for his aggrieved clients. That one, very visible, stand-out success has defined him as *the* class-action attorney for similar wrongful-death cases. By recognizing a golden opportunity and seizing a career-building moment, his practice, his personal and professional satisfaction, and his income have all skyrocketed beyond belief.

A few months after I began my career at the William Morris Agency, I was given the important assignment of writing all of the contracts and being the agency's business-affairs point person for the new morning *David Letterman Show*. This program would make William Morris a great deal of money in commissions. Upon receiving this assignment, I knew this would be a defining moment for me with my new employers. With this in mind, I busted my butt, spending late evenings and weekend time giving my best efforts right from the start. My hard work paid off big-time. David's managers were so pleased with how well things went that one of them—the legendary Jack Rollins—sent a letter to one of the heads of William Morris detailing how happy he and his client, David, were with my meticulousness, the amount of responsibility I had assumed, and how well I interacted with the show's staff members. All of this caused my William Morris career to get off to a positive and visible start, and I was accorded respect for my efforts.

My client Liz Claman set an excellent example of someone seizing an unexpected and potentially great opportunity when it came her way. When I first met Liz, she was an intern at a Los Angeles TV station. Because she is exceedingly bright, talented, and resourceful, she and her career enjoyed a rapid rise from being an intern to a reporter in Columbus, Ohio, to an Emmy Award–winning morning-show host in Cleveland, and then to a weekend anchor in Boston. It was when Liz was working in Boston that she shared her *Goal* with me that being an anchor/host on cable TV was the ideal next step in her career trajectory.

We now needed to figure out how Liz would attain her *Goal*. Shortly thereafter, I received a call from a CNBC executive who said that CNBC was looking for somebody with a unique skill set: They wanted a great communicator who could impart business news in an understandable way, someone who had an innate ability to connect with viewers, and someone who above all was smart. I called Liz with this information, and she immediately looked at it as a golden opportunity that she had not considered before. The more she thought about it, the more excited she became about making this substantial pivot in her career path.

Liz, who is very astute and a quick study, voraciously read and watched everything she could about the world of business over the next few days, as she didn't have a traditional business background. I then contacted CNBC to make the case for hiring her. CNBC agreed to meet with Liz and she nailed the interview. A week or so later, CNBC decided to hire and groom her as one of their weekday business news anchors. It didn't take long for Liz to shine and become a highly watched and very popular weekday anchor/host on CNBC. Today, years later, Liz may very well be the most well-respected woman in business news, as she hosts *The Claman Countdown* on the Fox Business Network.

Liz loves her extraordinary and highly fulfilling network career, and all this has happened because she, in the radiant spirit of *carpe diem*, was appropriately and skillfully opportunistic at the right time.

A home run that wins the World Series or a touchdown catch that decides the Super Bowl are much more success-evoking accomplishments than identical plays in preseason games. Not all moments or opportunities are equal! By recognizing golden opportunities and defining moments, and by making the most of them, you can put yourself on a far more rewarding track that can lead to huge future professional successes.

Once you recognize that you are facing a pivotal, game-changing, and game-enhancing moment, you must be opportunistic and make the most of it, as it may never come again. Just ask Dan Marino, the hall-of-fame quarterback who played in the Super Bowl once. His team, the Miami Dolphins, lost that game and he never made it back to the Super Bowl again.

In life, you may only get one shot to accomplish something great, so you must treat these opportunities as precious and do everything you can to secure a positive outcome.

Strata-Gems

1. Successful individuals are *opportunistic*. They sense defining moments and do their best to seize them, and then they work in a focused manner to bring about a successful result.

2. There are two components of being an effective, opportunistic choreographer. First, recognize when an extraordinary opportunity is being presented to you or can be created or initiated by you. Second, make the very most of the opportunity and do your best to secure a positive result.

28

IDENTIFY THE VOID
AND THE NEED IN THE
MARKETPLACE

I have counseled my clients that they can attain great success if they

1. identify a void and a need in the marketplace,

2. design a success-evoking choreography to take advantage of that void and need, and

3. effectively implement that choreography.

I can attest to the efficacy of these three steps, as I was one of the first talent representatives to seek out fledgling newscasters and program hosts in very small markets and fashion a business devoted to being their Career Choreographer. Up until that time, most companies only represented seasoned broadcast journalists who were already working at the networks or in large markets.

I learned about this void in the marketplace when I took my first trip as a young agent to San Diego, Sacramento, and San Antonio more than thirty-five years ago. Upon arriving in these cities, I found that only one of the twenty or so newscasters with whom I met was represented (a gaping void) and that there was a huge business potential in moving newscasters from small- and mid-sized markets to larger ones (a glaring need).

Immersing myself in this business, and being at the forefront of it, has served me incredibly well for the past three decades. During this time, person after person has remarked, "You have a great niche!"

Yes, I do. I'm very fortunate.

Additionally, I was the first representative to focus on developing newscasters to become hosts of reality-based shows such as *Access Hollywood*, *Extra*, *Dancing with the Stars*, and the like. Tapping into and filling this void and need has also served me, my clients, and my company very well.

When trying to identify a void and a need in a marketplace, some things to research and think about are

1. What is already being done—or has already been done—in the field at issue?

2. Is it being done—or has it been done—well? (If not, there may be both a void and a need.)

3. What isn't being done? (Is there a void in the marketplace?)

4. If there is a void, is there also a need? This is an important distinction. For our purposes, a void shall mean an opening or opportunity, something that's not yet been done, or done well, or something that doesn't yet exist. But just because there is a void doesn't mean there is also a need. There can be a huge void, but no great need (for what you want to do).

For example, let's go back to Danielle, the single mom and real estate broker who desperately wanted to stay in real estate during the economically troubled years of 2008 and 2009. She thought she found a void in the real estate market, as few, if any, brokers during the economic downturn were bringing high-end properties to individuals solely as investments. However, after doing her homework, she learned that during the dark days of the recession, there didn't appear to be a true need for this service. As a result, she decided to pursue her other *Goal* of working for a production company.

As an astute choreographer, you must honestly discern whether there is in fact a need for your proposed services or product that makes it worthwhile for you to devote your valuable time, energy, and resources to fulfilling that need. You must also consider if you are capable and qualified to fill a particular void and need or advance what has already been done in connection with an already-existing product or service.

Once again, if there is a void and a need in a given area, and you are qualified and excited to develop and implement an effective choreography that takes advantage of these golden opportunities, you put the percentages heavily in your favor that you will be successful. You also may well develop and enjoy empowering feelings of validation and high self-esteem from being an effective choreographer, visionary, and pioneer.

Years ago, I met with a psychologist whose specialty was family counseling. He was referred to me because he wanted to find a niche with great potential in his field so that he could write and speak about that niche, and thereby expand his practice.

As we talked, I learned that the majority of this psychologist's clients came to him because they were having marital problems. In these cases, his goals were to listen, learn, prod, suggest, and/or mitigate, and in the best of all worlds, alleviate the problem. He laughingly referred to himself as "Mr. Fix It" because each day, he was called upon to fix problems and cure marital ills.

During our conversation, he offhandedly made the remark that if these individuals had come to him with these issues *prior* to getting married, they would have avoided a great deal of angst and grief. He recently had been counseling a number of clients who were contemplating marriage, who had issues or potential problems they wanted to resolve beforehand, including the following:

1. One partner was getting cold feet about having children.

2. One partner, who initially was all for living in Los Angeles, now wanted to move home to Minneapolis, a city she perceived would be far better for raising a family and where the couple's earnings would go much further. The other partner had made a home in L.A., had established a lucrative business there, and didn't want to leave his base of operations.

3. One partner was Baptist, the other Jewish. In what religion(s) would their children be raised?

4. One partner was moving to Los Angeles to marry her fiancé and live with him and his son there. He had a beautiful home in L.A., which he had designed. He and his son loved the home and wanted to stay there. But his wife-to-be felt uncomfortable moving into "his" house. She wanted her fiancé to sell his house so they could buy a house both of them could decorate. Essentially, a new home, she perceived, would feel like "theirs."

All of these issues, the psychologist explained, had the potential, in time, to tear a marriage apart. My client then remarked that he loved pre-marriage counseling and found it to be very effective in working out potential problems before they became deal-breaking marriage-wreckers.

There it was! We struck niche gold! He could focus on and market himself as a preventive, pre-marriage counselor.

He loved the idea. He would specialize in "Potential Problem Prevention," in that his practice, writing, and speaking would primarily focus upon premarital problem prevention and problem solving.

Over the past years, my client's practice has grown way beyond his expectations. He is now writing his first book on premarital problem solving.

Another story involves "Cindy," a successful account executive for a top luxury-magazine publishing corporation. Cindy's job is to bring in new advertising accounts to the various national magazines that her company publishes. Up until the 2008 economic downturn, Cindy had been wildly successful at opening up new accounts for her company. But with so many companies severely cutting their advertising budgets, she was justifiably concerned that finding new, lucrative advertisers during the challenging 2008–2009 recession would be extremely difficult, at best.

During our discussions, we focused on whether the recession had created any new opportunities or niches that didn't exist before or were more attractive during this precarious new economic reality for potential or current magazine advertisers. At one point during our discussions, Cindy mentioned that she had just brought in a major high-end clothing chain as a new client—a company that she had been unable to make any headway with before. I asked Cindy why at this economically challenging time this company reversed course and decided to spend significant money advertising in her magazines. She replied, "They [the new client's executives] believe that with their competitors retreating from the advertising market due to cost-cutting, it was an ideal opportunity for them to reposition their chain of boutique stores with a major advertising blitz, and [thereby] secure a much larger share of a market that they are confident will come back."

My response to Cindy was that obviously this company saw a golden opportunity to increase their market share by doing *more* advertising during the recession. So I suggested that she follow their lead and go to the appropriate new and current advertisers with that same concept: "*Now*—while others are doing significantly less advertising—is the time to be aggressive and position yourself to take advantage of everyone else's fears and cutbacks by garnering a bigger piece of the market . . . because, as we all know, our economy *will* come back!"

Within four months of our conversation, Cindy re-created her sales pitch for many of her magazines' current and potential advertisers in such an effective way that, to the amazement of her senior management, she flourished during that very challenging economic time. In recognition of her creative reset and tremendous success, Cindy received a huge promotion and pay raise.

Just as Cindy found a beautiful oasis smack in the middle of the hot sands of the 2008–2009 economic downturn desert, you will be well served to figure out where the next big needs and opportunities are. In business, the one thing that remains constant is change, so it's always an ideal time to be the most creative and insightful new niche seeker, niche identifier, or niche creator possible. Do not get left behind in the race to find your place and success in our new business world.

Strata-Gems

1. One major key to attaining your *Goals* and *Dreams* is to identify whether there is a viable void and a need in the marketplace that you are excited about and capable of filling.

2. It is imperative that you distinguish between a void and a need, and that you're reasonably sure that both exist. There can be a void in the marketplace that, as a result of little or no need, does not demand or justify the use of your time, energy, and resources, or your pursuit. Do your research and be discerning.

FEAR

Fear can make you all uptight,
And scared to death to do what's right.
When you're paralyzed with fear,
You can't clearly see or hear.

And when you are afraid and scared,
Means of growth can be impaired.
So let there be no disparity,
Face life with crystal clarity.

And passionately pursue what you deem dear,
So that you can enjoy your best career!

—K.L.

29

DO NOT LET FEAR PARALYSIS IMPEDE OR DERAIL YOUR CAREER GROWTH

If you don't get out of the boat,
you'll never walk on water!

—UNKNOWN

If you see something you like [and it's highly beneficial],
you have to be able to pull the trigger [and go for it].

—JASON GARRETT,
former head coach of the Dallas Cowboys

Having courage as a Career Choreographer doesn't
mean that you don't have fear; it means that you
will rise above your fear and act in a highly
constructive and beneficial manner.

—K.L.

F ear is manifested in many ways, and it can lead you to make career-derailing choices. You can be so fearful of making a move, making a change, or taking a calculated risk that the fear paralyzes you, and you never make what could turn out to be a beneficial career step. Instead, you wind up in the debilitating, often demoralizing position of being mired in a career-halting limbo, or worse.

An illustration of this dynamic occurred with Danielle, the single mom with a failing real estate business during the 2008–2009 recession. She became frozen with fear due to the fact that she was no longer able to support herself and her son, and because she perceived that she had no option other than to take a soul-numbing bank position so she could have a steady, guaranteed income.

When Danielle and I began to discuss various potential choreographies, her terror began to subside, as she had a logical set of steps—a beneficial plan of action—from which she could identify potential new and exciting employment options. With a clear game plan in hand, she went from fear-ridden to empowered.

Trust me, achievers may well have fears, but they rise above them; these individuals don't let their anxiety preclude them from seeking beneficial change, taking a worthwhile risk, and seeing what's "out there," while astutely discerning whether the potential new choices are better than what they currently have.

As you can glean from the case of Danielle, one of the main means to allay or dissipate your career fears is to thoughtfully construct a logical and beneficial choreography, because with a plan comes clarity, confidence, direction, power, hope, and faith—all essential and beautiful *Goal-* and *Dream*-attainment gifts.

Another way that fear leads to highly destructive decision making is when you are so apprehensive regarding someone, something, or some (potential or hypothetical) event that you opt to unthinkingly make a self-sabotaging quick, reactive move, which will impede or preclude you from attaining your *Goals* and *Dreams*. In this instance, the powerful emotion of fear overwhelms and dismantles your best judgment, you lose all discipline, and you make a move that makes you feel better *for the moment* without having given any real thought to the long-term, deleterious consequences of opting for a quick-fix solution.

Fear can take many forms, such as fear of failure, fear of success (of being exposed as a "fraud," if you perceive that you don't have the necessary talents, skills, or knowledge to merit your success, or because your deeply ingrained insecurities make you feel undeserving of the success), or fear of change or the unknown. In connection with this last dynamic, I would like to share some relevant research.

Many years ago, I was told about an experiment that was conducted with mice in a cage in order to learn how they would react to facing the unknown. As I understand it, one-half of the cage floor on which all of the mice were standing was electrified. At various intervals, the feet of the mice were shocked, which made them jump and squeal in pain. After the mice received a series of shocks, the gate in the middle of the cage was opened so that the mice could flee to the other side, with the possibility that they could escape the shocks. The incredible result of this experiment was that *not one* mouse went over to the other side of the cage in order to avoid the shocks. For our purposes, at least two conclusions can be drawn from this study:

1. The fear of physical pain was preferred by or less daunting to the mice than was the *fear of the unknown* or the *fear of change*.

2. The fear of the unknown seemed to be intellectually crippling to the mice, as it appears to have caused them not to think or act rationally, which may be one reason why *not one* mouse ventured over to the other side of the cage to see if life over there would be less painful.

The moral of the story? Don't be like those mice and let your fears of the unknown or change shackle you and stall or destroy your career.

Throughout the thirty-plus years that I have owned my representation firm, I have counseled my staff members to not be afraid to approach newscasters and program hosts about our potentially representing them. So often, people fear taking a shot at something because they are afraid of being rejected and failing. This fear is absolutely career growth retarding and can be career-ending. In business, as in life, you can't be afraid to put yourself on the line, or, as the cliché goes, "You can't get a hit if you don't get up to bat."

I tell my staff members that "if you approach ten potential clients about representation, maybe two or three will at some point soon say yes, which would be a huge victory! Another two or three or more may not be ready to commit now, but in the years to come, with circumstances being different, they may remember their conversation with you and at that time choose to have you represent them. So, you now have between four and six clients that you wouldn't have had but for you rising above your fear of failure and rejection. Even if you just secure the representation of one client from your efforts, it's a plus, or even if you just let ten people in our business know how successful our clients have been with us, it's still a public-relations win. So be a courageous particle in motion and positively interact with other valuable particles in motion. Transcend your fears!"

Strata-Gems

1. Fear can debilitate and demoralize you spiritually, emotionally, and psychologically, and it can stall or decimate your career.

2. Individuals who attain their *Goals* and *Dreams* rise above their fears—they're not sabotaged by them.

3. Crafting an achievable choreography may well dissipate your feelings of fear. It will give you the clarity, direction, power, and confidence to attain your loftiest *Goals* and *Dreams*, and thereby enable you to actualize your fullest potential.

30

BE AN ENTREPRENEUR
FOR YOUR EMPLOYER

When I was assigned to work in the William Morris Agency news department, I took the initiative to identify and make the most of the untapped area of finding up-and-coming newscasters in small markets. During two weeks of my first vacation as a news agent, I went from city to city, watching local newscasts, and then contacting and securing the representation of several highly promising on-air individuals. By doing this, I built a business for my employer, which benefited me greatly and accelerated my growth within the company. A few years later, I moved from the William Morris New York City office to their Beverly Hills office. When I arrived there, they represented a few newscasters at that latter office. When I left the company four years later, the William Morris Beverly Hills office represented approximately 160 newscasters and hosts. During that time, I established that office as a major force in the newscaster representation arena, so all parties were big winners! Put another way, I was a proactive entrepreneur for my company.

Another example of a company entrepreneur is my client Mario Lopez. Becoming the host of *Extra* was one of Mario's *Dreams*. As the *Extra* host, Mario worked in a highly strategic and effective manner to make *Extra* significantly more successful. One way he accomplished this was to personally initiate and take trips throughout the country to meet with local TV station executives, whose stations air *Extra*. Mario did this in an effort to learn how he and the executives at Telepictures (which produces the show) could best serve the station and its viewership, and thereby increase ratings. Mario strategically collaborated with Telepictures' executives as a quasi-entrepreneur of *Extra* because he knew that the show's success was his success. Mario's entrepreneurial efforts did not go unnoticed or unrewarded by Telepictures executives, as Telepictures was exceedingly giving in allowing Mario to render services in connection with various outside properties—such as hosting the network show *X Factor*. Mario was also on occasion allowed to develop and produce potential shows on weekend episodes of *Extra*, which was a huge benefit for him.

Another example of being a wise and proactive entrepreneur for an employer involves my longtime weathercaster client Irv Gikofsky, who is lovingly known in New York City as "Mr. G." Over the years, Irv has helped bring in hundreds of thousands of dollars of ad revenue by introducing his station executives to potential advertisers. As a result of Mr. G's entrepreneurial, revenue-producing efforts, his relationship with company executives has become a very special and highly beneficial one.

The important point here is that when you are a creative and effective self-starting entrepreneur for your company, great things can happen for you and your career.

Strata-Gem

If you can be a proactive, creative, money-making entrepreneur for your company, you surely increase the percentages that you will enjoy gratifying growth, valuable rewards, and success there.

31

HOW TO DEAL WITH DEFEAT AND GET YOUR CAREER BACK ON TRACK

Failure is underrated!

—DON BROWNE,
member of the Broadcasting Hall of Fame

Before you learn to succeed, you must learn to fail.

—SHAQUILLE O'NEAL,
former All-Star NBA basketball player

*Put your setbacks in your mental and emotional
rear-view mirror, as you drive toward success.*

—K.L.

In a book devoted to attaining success, it is essential that we talk about the process of understanding and coping with defeats, disappointments, and rejection. Here's the deal: If you compete for success, you will inevitably suffer a number of setbacks, some of which will be morale- and self-esteem-crushing. It's just the way it is. One key for recovery is to not let setbacks debilitate you or impede your long-term progress and success.

I believe that everyone who is successful has suffered demoralizing setbacks and spirit-deflating rejection, and/or been told at one point or another that they couldn't or wouldn't accomplish their *Goals.* My dad, for example, could barely speak English and was fired from his first department-store receiving-room position. For years, career-building doors slammed in his face. What all of these highly successful individuals apparently did after experiencing devastating defeats or rejection was to

1. Never, ever stop believing in themselves, even if it seemed as if everyone else had.

2. Absorb and survive the confidence-jarring body blows.

3. Try to learn as much as possible from the defeat (i.e., was there something they could correct or improve upon to avoid suffering another defeat in a similar situation?).

4. Get back in the game as soon as possible, with more effective strategies and improved choreographies, because if you don't get back in it—you have no chance to win it! You must suffer losses and setbacks and know how to lose and constructively rebound in order to attain ultimate and sustained success.

5. Put your detractors and setbacks in your mental and emotional rear-view mirror as you drive toward success.

I counsel my clients that defeats and setbacks and what one learns from them can well turn out to be strong first steps to securing wonderful victories and successes. Here are a few "how to get back on track" stories. I hope you find them instructive, motivating, and confidence-building.

THE "BABY-STEP" APPROACH

Years ago, I counseled a man named "Jordan," who was forty years old and lived in Seattle. He was well educated, bright, worldly, and had, at a young age, played a major role in building an Internet company that, at one point, was allegedly worth approximately five hundred million dollars. However, because of the alleged greed, fraudulent practices, and unscrupulous behavior of his partners—resulting in him having to bring an ugly lawsuit against them and pay out tremendous legal fees—he escaped the company with a relatively small amount of money and deep feelings of betrayal.

According to Jordan, for the next few years he was emotionally "shell-shocked and frozen." He literally could do nothing. With his confidence and motivation levels at an all-time low, he tried to help heads of fledgling companies raise capital—as he had so successfully done for his company a few years earlier. But, because his self-image and self-esteem were so very low, he didn't have the confidence to ask for an agreement memorializing the position that he would hold or even inquire about what he would earn with the new company if he were successful at raising the necessary capital. Instead, he felt like he had to continually prove his worth; otherwise, no one would give him an opportunity to show what he could do. But, by not having reached any kind of agreement before rendering his capital-raising services, Jordan set himself up for more failure and betrayal. And, unfortunately, in various ways, all of these companies wound up taking advantage of his insights, connections, and great work, and then they simply "dissed" him. Not one company paid Jordan anything near what his work was worth. In fact, one company allegedly paid him nothing (!), even though he introduced senior management to someone who ultimately was a source of substantial capital. And none of these companies kept him on once he had helped them. These setbacks further demoralized and paralyzed him. In fact, for the next five years, he couldn't even complete a work résumé.

After listening intently to Jordan over the course of a few conversations, I learned that he had been a foster child and that none of the many individuals he had lived with growing up had expressed any genuine love or given him any self-esteem-building approval. Some foster parents denigrated him, as well as shot down nearly every project that he undertook. It didn't take a rocket scientist to figure out why Jordan had no core confidence, why he suffered with deep feelings of low self-esteem, and why he consistently put himself in situations that were destined to fail.

In order to begin to jump-start Jordan's career, I asked him to fill out some *Clarifying Lists*. In seeing these, I discovered that he had a great track record of raising large sums of capital from both domestic and international sources, and he spoke three foreign languages fluently. He was also adept and accomplished at creating and implementing successful business models for new companies. Additionally, I learned that Jordan's true passion was to be involved in film development and production.

I asked Jordan whether he had any background in film, and he replied that he didn't—but he had always been an avid film viewer. I also inquired as to whether he would be willing to use his capital-raising skills and connections in his quest to get into the film industry. He said he would, but not for the long term.

After contemplating the situation, Jordan and I devised a choreography that focused on him taking calculated baby steps for a while, just so he could garner some small—but very much needed—intellect- and emotion-buoying victories, and build some based-on-success core confidence.

Within a couple of months, Jordan secured a low-paying job reading scripts for a film-production company. This baby step was just what the doctor ordered. He loved his work, and his employers loved him. Seven months later, he received a promotion. Within the next year, he was promoted twice more.

About three years into his job, Jordan was introduced to a successful and wealthy businessman who was CEO of a major communications company. This CEO's *Goal* was to buy or build a film-production and distribution company. After learning about Jordan's international capital-raising accomplishments and his production experience, he hired Jordan to help oversee his film-production company. For the past five years, Jordan has identified and helped produce several major films. His confidence has grown by leaps and bounds, and he is step by step becoming a successful and well-respected film executive. He loves, loves, loves his work, and feels much better about himself, his abilities, and his future.

Then there's the inspiring story of Janet Shamlian, whom I discovered over thirty years ago as an up-and-coming reporter in Grand Rapids, Michigan. After a few stops, Janet moved to Houston as an anchor and a reporter. In Houston, she met and married her husband. A year or so later, she stopped working and, over time, gave birth to five beautiful children.

Janet stayed out of broadcasting for seven years, trying to be the most attentive mother possible. Then one day, she called to tell me that she wanted to go back to work. However, like millions of individuals who have left the workforce for many years to raise their children, Janet had strong concerns that she was too old and had been out of the business for too long. She believed that having five children at home meant that going back to work was nothing more than a pipe dream.

I told her that it wasn't. But then she hit me with the real challenge! She didn't want to return to work as a freelance reporter for a local Houston station. Instead, she wanted to work for the NBC, ABC, or CBS network. In essence, she wanted to return from a seven-year absence and be given the *plum* position of being a national news correspondent in Houston—a city that didn't even have a network news bureau. Brutal!

Upon first blush, I told Janet that what she was asking for was exceedingly difficult to attain, but I'd think about how to develop a choreography that would allow her to live her *Dream*. However, Janet had already given her Comeback Choreography a great deal of thought and shared four excellent baby steps with me to begin her quest:

1. I would call the network recruiters and tell them about Janet and her desire to work for their network's news division.

2. While reporting in Chicago years earlier, Janet had worked with Lester Holt and Rob Stafford, both of whom work for the NBC network and are held in high regard there. Janet would call Lester and Rob and ask if they could put in calls of recommendation for her.

3. Janet would be proactive and pay for her own trip to New York City so she could meet with the network recruiters, show them that she still looked young and fit, and tell them that she was hungry to travel and report.

4. I would contact the recruiters to convince them to meet with Janet while she was in New York (which they all agreed to do).

Janet made a great presentation to the recruiters, especially to the NBC News executives, and she aced a writing test. After the meetings, ABC and CBS said they were impressed with Janet, but they didn't currently have anything for her. NBC, however, was a bit more encouraging, as they told us that they would try to use Janet when they had a need.

During the ensuing months, Janet kept in tasteful contact with the recruiters by sending emails reminding them that she was ready to report at their beck and call. Baby step by baby step, she made sure she stayed in the recruiters' thoughts.

Then, one day, she received a call from an NBC News producer who expressed a possible need for her to cover a story near Houston. Janet said she was ready, at any time, to go anywhere. Unfortunately, the producer then called back saying that she was no longer needed.

Several very long weeks went by. Then, another call came, and this time Janet got her shot to report for NBC. By all accounts, she did a wonderful job. Soon after, for minimal pay, NBC began to use Janet more and more to travel—at a moment's notice, for extended periods of time—and report from all over the country. Janet, to her credit, never declined an assignment, even though some required her to be available with just several moments' notice, with no time-line for when she would be finished and able to return to her family.

After a couple of months, Janet received a four-year contract with NBC News. What a spectacular success for a mom of five children who had been out of the workforce for more than seven years, and yet never lost faith that with appropriate, creative baby steps, she would revive her career and amazingly take it to a much, much higher level!

But wait, there's more! After being a prominent reporter for NBC News for many years, Janet and NBC parted ways. One might think that after accomplishing her *Dream* of being a major network news correspondent, Janet would have called it quits, but she still hungered to continue to do what she loved. So she called me and said that she wanted to choreograph one more major come-back, and we immediately got started mapping out our steps.

As we did years earlier, we contacted the network news divisions to see if there were any positions that were right for Janet, but there were no takers. We once again told the network recruiters that Janet would freelance for them to show how valuable she could be for them; however, no one bit. Many months passed, and there was dead silence. Through it all, I always felt that CBS News was the right fit for Janet's return, as they truly coveted seasoned and gifted storytellers.

About a year later, with Janet and I tastefully staying in touch with Laurie Orlando, a senior CBS vice president, Janet received a call from a CBS executive asking if she could fill in as a correspon-dent during the winter holiday. Sensing the fantastic opportunity, Janet said "absolutely" and then changed all of her holiday plans. Once again, things went smashingly well. Thereafter, CBS execu-tives called on Janet regularly, and within three months they offered her an excellent staff correspondent employment agreement, which she accepted.

Incredibly, against many odds and obstacles, Janet, who is a supremely talented and successful choreographer, made a second comeback! Congratulations, Janet, I have so much respect for you!

What you can take away from Janet's story is that if you create the most logical and success-evoking steps, you will be able to accom-plish many of your most treasured *Goals* and live your *Dreams*.

THE "SAFE HARBOR" APPROACH

Years ago, a newscaster named "Wendy" anchored and reported in a small Western market. Because of her extraordinary on-camera ease and presence, she immediately moved to a much larger mar-ket. However, due to her impatience with delayed gratification and a self-imposed and unrealistic success timetable, she left her middle-market news job way too soon and went to report for a TV station in Los Angeles—which she wasn't prepared for. She then made an unsuccessful move to a national show. Soon thereafter, Wendy suffered the major self-esteem blow of being fired by that show and having her termination written about in the major Los Angeles newspapers. Talk about public humiliation—this was it! To add insult to injury, no one would hire her after that. She went jobless for more than eight months. As time passed, she barely had any money to live on.

Needless to say, Wendy's confidence was in shambles. When she came to me for career coaching and representation, I told her that I could probably put together a demo tape that would get her a position on a national entertainment show or once again at a top-market local station, but that would be the absolute worst thing that I could do for her. What she needed to do was to go down in market size and find a "safe harbor"—that is, a local-market station that would embrace her and appreciate what she could bring to them. Essentially, she needed to get away from all the pressure and critics in Los Angeles and, baby step by baby step, rebuild her journalistic foundation, and more important, her self-esteem. After three years or so, she could then return to Los Angeles or to a national show with guns blazing and her confidence and skill sets unshakable.

In time, we found the ideal smaller-market position for Wendy, which she accepted. After a few months there, Wendy's employers loved her, telling her that she "walks on water." Wendy's confidence level grew stronger with each live show that she hosted. And thankfully, in this instance, she didn't grow impatient before it was the appropriate time to leave her safe harbor. As a result, the broadcasting world became her oyster, as many top employers sought her out for wonderful on-air positions.

Strata-Gems

1. There are many effective strategies you can use to rebound from a career setback or hiatus. Taking confidence-building baby steps and identifying and making the most of safe-harbor positions, at which you can secure earned confidence and self-esteem-building victories, are two excellent approaches.

2. There are no career failures—just valuable learning experiences that are necessary for you to attain future sweet career successes.

32

EMOTIONAL EQUILIBRIUM AND THE ART OF "SELECTIVE AMNESIA"

If you can meet with Triumph and Disaster,
And treat those two imposters just the same,
Yours is the Earth and everything that's in it.

—RUDYARD KIPLING

YOU control your thoughts, your emotions, your
confidence, your beliefs, your attitude, and your actions!
So stay cool, constructive, and in control.

—K.L.

One of the valuable lessons I learned as an athlete and have shared with clients is not to get too high when you win or too low when you suffer a setback. The key is to maintain your composure, poise, intellectual clarity, and perspective, while continuing to learn from both experiences.

If you get too high when you secure a victory, you may not

remain grounded, focused, hardworking, and conscientious. You may lose the edge that enabled and catalyzed you to secure the victory in the first place. Conversely, we have all seen or heard of athletes or individuals in other professions who suffer a setback, lose confidence, and wind up mired in an emotional pothole from which they can't extricate themselves. As a result, they suffer many more setbacks during their slump. As we have discussed, the key for all competitors in the business/professional world is to understand and embrace that, along the way, you will suffer defeats and reversals. Everyone loses. Your goals as a brilliant Career Choreographer are to pick yourself up from the deck, dust yourself and your confidence off, understand why you didn't secure a victory in this instance, take the essential steps to shore up the weak spots in your game, and move on to put yourself in the best position to secure cherished victories in the future—hopefully sooner rather than later.

There are some things you can't control. However, you do control your thoughts, emotions, confidence, beliefs, attitude, and actions! So stay constructive and in control.

The key is to learn from the past and not be brought down by it. Many years ago, a relief pitcher for the Los Angeles Dodgers was brought into a World Series game in the ninth inning, with the Dodgers winning 4–3. There were runners on second and third base, with one out. On the second pitch, the batter hit a line drive that caromed off the outfield wall, driving in both runners, for the game-winning hit. It was a brutal ending for the Dodgers and that relief pitcher, as he very publicly and dramatically failed to do his job that day. The next day, that same relief pitcher was brought in once again in the ninth inning, with runners on first and third; the Dodgers were winning the game at that point, 3–2. This time, the relief pitcher was able to induce the batter to hit into an inning-ending double play. The Dodgers won in part because that pitcher did his job effectively.

I will always remember the post-game interview with that pitcher. When he was asked how he was able to come back that day and do such a stellar job, after failing to protect the Dodgers' precious lead the day before, he responded that he just totally put yesterday's loss out of his mind so it wouldn't impede or distract him from saving the game today. Essentially, he said that he develops a sort of "amnesia" so he doesn't go into a destructive funk or slump after a setback or loss. Similarly, I've seen Roger Federer, probably the best male tennis player ever, rebound brilliantly after suffering a devastating loss. It's clear that Federer has mastered the highly beneficial art of "selective amnesia."

The reason I call this essential tool in your psychological and emotional arsenal *selective amnesia* is because there are two dynamics at play here. The first is that you want to be able to effectively move on from or move past a setback—this is the amnesia component. But you also want to objectively and honestly assess why things didn't go well for you in the situation at hand. This way, you can identify the problem, learn from it, and choose a more success-evoking strategy and set of behaviors for the future. So you are selective, in the sense that, on the one hand, you want to forget the setback so it doesn't impede you, bring you down, or hold you back in the future, but on the other hand, you want to remember what you learned from this apparent "negative" experience so that you can improve and grow from it. So you selectively choose what to remember and what not to remember from an apparent setback. Finally, the reason I use the word "apparent" before the words "negative experience" and "setback" is because I have consistently shared with my clients, throughout my thirty-five years of career counseling, that if viewed constructively, failures can be your first beautiful steps to securing many sweet and highly rewarding victories in the future. So please remember, losing or not succeeding is an integral part of the life process; the key is to constructively use those setbacks as a means to learn, to grow, and to improve yourself and your professional life strategies.

Strata-Gems

1. Do not get too high or too low in connection with your successes and setbacks, respectively. It is essential, as a success-evoking choreographer, to stay focused, conscientious, poised, and in your very best frame of mind to secure many more successes.

2. The art of practicing "selective amnesia" requires you to forget or put aside your apparent losses or setbacks while remembering the lessons you've learned from these experiences; thereafter, you efficaciously use this knowledge in future situations as a means to secure sweet and coveted victories.

THE LOYALTY AND
FAMILIARITY FACTORS

My dad, Jack, served in the army for more than three years during World War II and took away many wonderful and insightful stories from his overseas experiences. The one that stands out for me involves Jack's Kentucky platoon-mate Charlie. As Jack tells it, Charlie was scrawny, clumsy, and socially awkward. Sadly, many of the men in camp played jokes on Charlie and poked fun at him. Jack, having repeatedly been an underdog himself, felt sorry for Charlie and chose him as a buddy. When Jack and Charlie were both picked to go overseas, Jack told Charlie not to worry, as Jack—who was fit and strong—would take care of him. Charlie was sincerely grateful and thanked Jack profusely, as Charlie was neither athletic nor physically gifted. As Charlie himself put it, he was much more of a "bookworm."

But you couldn't judge this bookworm by his cover! One evening, Jack and Charlie were in deserted North African hill country, walking back from a town, when some huge wild dogs began to run toward them. Jack's first instinct was to turn and run. Charlie immediately stopped him and, in a whisper, warned, "Jack, don't move! They'll tear you to shreds if you run. Do exactly what I'm doing. Pick up some dirt and hold it, as if you're going to throw it in their eyes. But don't throw it. Just stand still."

As the dogs drew closer, they began to bark and snarl more viciously. Charlie quickly got in front of Jack, acting as a human shield. When the dogs were nearly upon them, Charlie held up his fist, as if he were going to throw the dirt. The dogs stopped in their tracks. A moment or so later, they resumed moving forward, ready to attack. Once again, Charlie raised his fist full of dirt, as if to throw it. The dogs backed up. Charlie whispered to a terrified Jack, who was standing right behind him, "Don't move!" Charlie picked up more dirt. He once again acted as if he were going to throw it at the dogs. Finally, the dogs backed away, turned, and left.

That night, Charlie may well have saved Jack's life. He had shown great loyalty in return for the loyalty that Jack had given to him.

When it comes to the world of business, I have seen, over and over again, how people's careers have risen to incredible heights because of loyalty. For example, when my dad trained his buyers during his first career working for the J. W. Mays department-store chain, he remained faithful to the ones who were talented, productive, and loyal to him. When my dad was "retired" by Mays and out of work for three years thereafter, it was Ben Cammarata, one of my dad's former stellar trainees and the eventual chairman of the board of the TJX Companies, who hired him to train the buyers of his new department-store chain, T.J. Maxx.

Throughout the next twenty-nine years, my dad remained intensely loyal to (and exceedingly productive for) Ben. And Ben, during this time, returned the loyalty. So much so, in fact, that when my dad, at eighty-eight, decided to move with my mom to Los Angeles, he fully expected T.J. Maxx to ask him to retire. But, much to his surprise, the company paid for their move and even arranged to have my dad taken to work by town car and then dropped off three days a week for the next ten years. During this hugely successful time for both Ben and my dad, Ben rewarded my dad with raises and bonuses, so that my dad would know how much T.J. Maxx appreciated his contributions.

When my dad was nearly ninety-eight, Ben decided to step back from running the day-to-day operations of T.J. Maxx. It was also time for my dad to graciously and gratefully end a beautiful career—a career that flourished way beyond anybody's reasonable expectations, in great part because of the loyalty that Ben and my dad had to each other.

When I left the William Morris Agency to form my own company, two of the talented individuals whom I believed in and were loyal to me immediately became integral members of my firm. When Jim Wyatt, the co-president of the respected talent agency International Creative Management, left that firm to become CEO of the William Morris Agency, he took a number of experienced and loyal individuals with him. The same thing can be said for the brilliant news executive Dennis Swanson, who was credited with giving Oprah Winfrey her true career-launching talk show. As Dennis went from ABC to NBC to CBS and then to Fox, he hired and promoted a good number of the executives who had been loyal to him through the years.

A close friend of mine, "Annie," after working for her insurance company as an investor for twenty-eight years, needed to find a new job at age fifty-seven, as she had been laid off during the 2008–2009 economic downturn. The problem, as she posed it, was this: "Who would hire someone nearly fifty-eight years old for an executive position in our economy?" I strongly suggested that she contact all of the executives who had worked with and for her over the years, as well as other executives in the industry who were familiar with the high caliber of her work.

Because Annie was excellent at what she did, was a hard worker, and had been respectful to everyone, two executives she contacted, with whom she had worked through the years, offered her positions—one of which was perfect for her, which she accepted!

In Annie's case—much like my dad's—it was unlikely, as the result of her age, that she would be offered an executive position through normal employment-securing channels. But in both instances, Annie and my dad were able to extend their careers with wonderful positions that were created for them by people who knew, respected, and valued them.

There are a plethora of stories in the business world of how people have hitched their wagons and their career fortunes to others and stayed loyal to them. As a result of this loyalty and familiarity (and because these individuals were also talented), they have enjoyed rewarding career growth, success, and longevity.

Strata-Gems

1. Choosing talented and loyal individuals to be loyal to in return can contribute—possibly in a major way—to your long-term career success.

2. When looking for a new position, seek out those individuals who can hire you, or are in positions of influence, who are familiar with your good work and strong character.

34

BE A RESPECTFUL LISTENER AND A CONFIDENT, RELAXED COMMUNICATOR

A rtfully communicating and forging a *positive* and *impactful* connection with those with whom you're speaking are invaluable skills in business. In many ways, communicating and connecting with others is much like interviewing in the news and hosting professions. One of the skills I look for and appreciate when I watch someone conduct an interview is whether the interviewer truly listens to what the interviewee gives her or him, and whether the interviewer then organically and appropriately responds to it.

The best interviewers are *respectful listeners*. However, sometimes one isn't an effective interviewer not because of disrespectful listening, but because he or she is focused on other things and may barely be listening. This can happen when an interview is too scripted with prepared questions. As a result, once the interviewee finishes an answer, the interviewer immediately, mechanically, and unthinkingly goes on to ask the next prepared question—regardless of the interviewee's response. When this happens, a wonderful nugget of information, which might need further examination or elucidation, is dismissed or glossed over. Not only does this tightly scripted interview feel lifeless to the viewers, but it also feels vacuous and pedestrian to the interviewee. An unmemorable interview and interaction are often the end results for all involved.

It is the truly confident and relaxed interviewer who lets an interview breathe and then respectfully seizes moments of truth and beauty, thereby making the most of them. The same thing can be said about an artful conversationalist.

There are a number of reasons why someone can appear to be a disrespectful listener and an unartful interviewer:

1. The interviewer or communicator is nervous or scared, and rigidly sticks to the prepared set of questions as a safety net.

2. The interviewer or communicator is so uninvolved or dispassionate about some component of the interview that this lack of interest in the interviewee or the interview's subject matter is reflected by the interviewer's lack of respectful listening or nonresponsive questions.

3. The interviewer or communicator is absorbed in himself or his own agenda and isn't focused on being a giving and respectful listener and interviewer.

An example of this third reason for disrespectful listening occurred years ago with a quick-witted host named "Chris." Chris's career got off to a relatively slow start, but he received a great deal of positive attention when he became the host of a groundbreaking new local station morning show. On that program, his razor-sharp wit and comedic timing made him stand out as he delivered the news of the day. As a result, he in the best of all ways broke through the clutter of "vanilla" local-market hosts and anchors.

A couple of years later, Chris was given the coveted position of hosting a major cable network late-night interview program. The problem was that Chris was used to playing everything for the laugh as an anchor of his news show, and he just assumed the same strategy would work for his interviews. It didn't. When his guests would attempt to answer one of his questions, Chris would often interrupt them and interject a joke or a sarcastic remark—before the guest had finished answering. In essence, Chris was so intently focused on making each moment his own, instead of his guest's, that he was perceived by many to be a selfish and self-indulgent non-listener. Obviously, neither quality is attractive or endearing either on-air or in business communications.

By sticking to his always-go-for-the-joke-at-every-opportunity strategy, which worked for him as an anchor/host but was totally inappropriate in the role of an interviewer, Chris found that things quickly began to go south for him. I believe that this destructive behavior served as a defense mechanism for Chris. By always making quick jokes and not allowing any real connection to be forged, he avoided developing any real intimacy with his guests. But it was not until a couple of months after he had become the host of the cable network interview show—and "A-list" guests and viewers began to dwindle at a precipitous rate—that Chris finally got the message: If you want to connect with someone, show them that you respect them and that you truly desire to hear what it is that they are telling you. The key is to be an open, objective, and active listener.

Another way for an interviewer to respect an interviewee is to show that she or he has done the necessary research and homework regarding the interviewee by asking questions on the basis of the relevant information gleaned and secured from that research—rather than relying solely on the "cheat sheets" provided by a show's producer or researcher. This extra effort may go a long way toward establishing an extra-special rapport and connection with the interviewee, enabling the interviewer to elicit far more personal information from the interviewee than would otherwise be the case.

An example of this beneficial extra effort took place when Harry Smith, then-host of *The Early Show*, interviewed actress Amanda Peet. Obviously, when an actor or actress is on a pre-film-release press tour, the interviewee expects to be asked questions focusing on the new film. But instead of asking questions that Ms. Peet had either heard ten times before or that she had anticipated, Harry took a different path. He analogized and compared her role in her new film to that in one of her early films, which he had obviously taken time to personally research and watch. As a direct result of Harry's offbeat but highly insightful questions, the Amanda Peet interview turned into a magical experience for Peet, Harry, and the audience. Literally, Ms. Peet appeared to be tickled pink that Harry knew so much about her early work. It made for a truly insightful conversation to listen to and watch. Additionally, they forged a beautiful connection, and thereafter, Ms. Peet reportedly looked forward to being interviewed by Harry.

When I remarked to an *Early Show* staff member that I thought Harry's interview with Ms. Peet was great, the staff member shared that "Harry always tries to find something unusual about or especially meaningful to his interviewee, as a way to strike a personal chord with them."

What a great lesson for all communicators! Make an extra effort to learn something unique and specific about the person with whom you will be speaking, in a true and honest effort to be a respectful listener as well as an artful communicator. When it comes to having fruitful, engaging, and positively impactful professional communications, you often get out what you put in. So be an active and well-prepared communicator, as well as an open, interested, and respectful listener. In all likelihood, you will lay the groundwork to be much more successful in all of your professional interactions.

Strata-Gems

1. If you aspire to have positive and impactful professional communications, it is essential that you develop the art of being an open, active, interested, and respectful listener.

2. If you want to connect and forge a relationship with someone, if at all possible, learn things about them beforehand as a means to facilitate a meaningful conversation.

35

DEVELOP AN ENGAGING, SUCCESS-EVOKING PERSONALITY

Develop a personality that fits your business and makes people want to work with you.

—JACK LINDNER

Next door to a popular Los Angeles deli, a small, nondescript shoe-shine shack called Jack's Polished Act operated for many years. Soleme, its longtime proprietor, had the warmest, most winning personality and the brightest smile imaginable. When Soleme smiled and greeted you by your first name, it was like radiant sunshine breaking through on a cloudy day. It was motivating and contagious! Through the years, he became a neighborhood institution.

A few years ago, as I was dropping off my shoes with Soleme, my friend Dave was picking up two pairs of his. As Dave and I walked down the block, I asked him why he didn't use the very competent shoe-shine man conveniently located in the office building where Dave and I worked. Dave matter-of-factly answered, "You know, Soleme's just such a nice guy. I guess I save my shoes for him 'cause I just like him. My whole family brings their shoes to him."

Dave articulated my feelings exactly. Soleme did a fine job shining shoes, but so did the man in our building. But Dave and scores of other locals made the extra effort to bring their shoes to Soleme because of the effervescent and sincere manner in which he greeted and talked with us. *He made us want to do business with him.*

Soleme's is a simple story that encompasses a profound truth and career lesson: In most instances, when the product or services involved are comparable, people will want to do business with and gravitate toward those individuals whom they like, enjoy dealing with, and trust. It makes sense, right? So it also makes perfect sense that if you want to be successful at your job and in your career, it is essential to have (or to develop) a personality that leads people to want to work and do business with you.

For years, I overheard my dad instruct his buyer-trainees to develop a warm, relaxed personality that makes people feel comfortable and at ease. He'd frequently finish this thought by saying, "Remember, you get more bees with honey than with vinegar!"

I have found my dad's advice to be consistently effective when forming relationships, advancing and closing deals, and getting people to want to talk, meet, and do business with me and my clients. I'll never forget the visual example my dad gave when discussing how he, like the most skilled surgeon, artfully extracted advantages in a negotiation from an individual who initially had no intention of granting certain financial requests:

> When you negotiate, Kenny, the key is to be the most artful, precise, amiable, and gentle surgeon possible. When I negotiate with a manufacturer, we trade fun stories that resonate and laugh about "The Business," while I ever-so-gently make an incision. We talk about our mutual friends as I gently cut. Then we discuss our families—especially our kids. I make one or two

more snips. And before you know it, the negotiation's over. We've had a wonderful conversation, and I've gotten fifteen percent off what we paid the last time! *Remember*, just as surgeons can't do their best work when they're rigid, nervous, or scared, when you negotiate, be relaxed, and thereby relax others. You'll be far more successful!

This self-evident philosophy is one big reason why my dad was hired at age sixty-nine, and was kept on for nearly thirty more years, by the Marmaxx Operating Corp. (Marshall's & T.J. Maxx) to teach T.J. Maxx buyers how to negotiate advantageous deals, open up new resources, and repair or rekindle damaged and dormant relationships. Whenever I'd meet a manufacturer with whom my dad did business, they'd say, with great feeling and admiration: "I *love* being beaten up by your dad when we negotiate. He knows everything about the market, he's fun and easy to be with, he's respectful, and he always knows just how far to push and when to let up!"

Daniel Goleman, in his book *Emotional Intelligence*, makes a compelling case that, oftentimes, individuals with high IQs (intelligence quotients) don't fare as well in real-life situations as individuals who have high *emotional intelligence* quotients.[12] I wholeheartedly agree. Individuals who do well in life and in business are often able—through their personality, good sense of people, and proficient social skills—to bring people to them. They facilitate the growth of positive and productive relationships.

That said, there is an important point to be made here: Personality, charisma, and great people skills are invaluable assets, but you must also have the goods, services, and skills that people

---

12   Daniel Goleman, *Emotional Intelligence: Why It Can Matter More Than IQ* (New York: Bantam, 2005).

want or need—or else the most wonderful personality won't mean a thing! The primary reason why station, program, and network news executives ultimately do business with me is because I can help them by bringing them many of this country's most talented, likable, and respected broadcast journalists—which in turn increase their shows' viewership and advertising revenues. The reason why people negotiated deals with my dad and T.J. Maxx is because T.J. Maxx has more than eight hundred stores (so they have huge buying power), and they pay their bills on time.

On the other hand, let me share another personality story with you. When I was a teenager, a new charismatic tennis instructor named "Ted" was hired at the tennis courts I frequented for many of my teenage years. Ted, who came from the South, had a big, bright, warm smile and an infectious laugh. Unquestionably, Ted brought a little bit of sunshine and optimism to everyone with whom he came into contact. For his first few weeks, people flocked to take lessons from Ted—much to the dismay and despair of the other club tennis pros. And, as Ted tossed ball after ball to his pupils, he was constantly encouraging—even when his pupils swatted ball after ball on a fly, over ten-foot-high fences. It's fair to say that some of the forehands launched during Ted's lessons still haven't landed! It turned out that Ted didn't know diddly about the correct tennis grips, stance, or swing. He just had great charisma. However, when, after weeks of lessons, none of his students improved, many got worse, and some contracted serious cases of tennis elbow, his engaging personality and smile weren't nearly enough to sustain his business. As dramatically as Ted had made his successful debut at our club, his pupils left him just as quickly—much to the delight of the other club pros. As Ted couldn't make ends meet teaching tennis, we never saw or heard from him again.

The moral of the story is that a winning personality can open up many valuable doors and initially bring in business, but you must have the necessary talents and goods to sustain your success.

Strata-Gem

Having great people skills can be invaluable in your quest to attain success, but this advantage must be combined with the requisite knowledge, skill sets, "goods," and abilities. If you have all of these assets, you can be a world-beater!

SPIN AND INTERNAL RATIONALIZATIONS

It takes the greatest discipline,
Not to use internal "spin."
"Spin" convinces us that what's wrong seems right,
And that escaping the truth, is quite all right.
When rationalizations are engaged,
Guilty feelings are assuaged.
But it doesn't take a master sleuth,
To discover deep down, we know the truth,
That rationalizations and "spin" both supply
Ways to live with internal lies.
"Spin" distorts the truth, with the greatest stealth,
Risking our growth and our mental health.
So if we want to make our very best choices,
We must listen to our inner voices.
And resist the urge, to begin,
Burying the truth, and concocting "spin."

—K.L.

36

DON'T RATIONALIZE AWAY CAREER-DESTRUCTIVE BEHAVIOR

Hindsight isn't 20/20 if you rewrite history in your mind or repress or ignore valuable truths.

—K.L.

A newscaster client of mine recently had an opportunity to play a small role in a feature film. In successfully conveying to me how dead set she was on appearing in the movie, she said, "I'm doing this [role] no matter what! I know that you are going to tell me that my contract says that I'm supposed to get permission from the station [her employer] in order to do it, but screw them! The last time we asked for permission, it took them so long to get back to us that we lost the darn role without ever learning whether they'd grant permission. We did it the right way then, and we got shafted. So this time, I'm doing it without asking them. I'll worry about it later. As they say, I'd rather ask for forgiveness than permission."

Okay, here are the facts, the issue, and my client's highly flawed reasoning. This client made over $250,000 annually by anchoring the news for her station. The thirty-second appearance in the film paid her $1,500. She had a contract with her station that prohibited her from doing all outside activities unless she first secured permission from her station.

My client's justifications for accepting the role without getting station management permission were that she really wanted it, and that the last time that she had asked for permission, she lost out on the opportunity.

My client passionately and righteously argued that the station had previously acted badly or insensitively, so this time, she wouldn't let them blow it for her again. Essentially, she *rationalized* that she had a moral "free pass" to ignore the crystal-clear prohibition in her contract regarding her acceptance of any outside employment opportunities.

My counsel to her was "I vehemently disagree! Inappropriate or insensitive acts by your employer, clients, or associates do *not* give you the justification to commit wrong, inappropriate, or career-diminishing or destructive acts yourself. One does not excuse or justify the other. Don't let someone else's bad or flawed behavior trigger destructive behavior on your part."

Against my advice, my client didn't ask permission before playing the role. And when her news manager caught wind of her appearance, he hit the proverbial roof. After some lengthy upper-management meetings, the news director called to tell me that *normally* my client would be subject to being fired the next time she materially breached her contract.

"However, the bigger issue," he continued gravely, "is that we've decided that this is not an isolated incident, and life's too short to have to deal with this kind of behavior. She was on the bubble anyway, so where we probably would have offered her a new, two-year guaranteed contract when this one ends—at $280,000 for the first year and $300,000 for the second—we're going to pass. Your client is free to quietly look for a [new] job. Sorry."

The manager continued by saying, "Want to talk about blowing it! Your client just lost a guaranteed $580,000 for what? A few thousand bucks to get her ego stroked?"

I then explained that the reason why my client didn't seek permission in this instance was her valid concern that the station management, as in the past, wouldn't respond quickly enough for her to accept the film producer's offer before the deadline.

The manager responded, "Kenny, it's our contractual right to be able to decide what outside activities your client can do. The station group manager was on vacation last time, and no one under him wanted to take the responsibility for giving the okay for that appearance. So we had to wait for him to return before we could give you an answer. I told your client the reason why we were slow to respond. But, in any event, our tardiness doesn't allow or warrant your client to violate her contract."

The manager ended our conversation with a stone-cold truth: "Your client gambled that we wouldn't find out about her role in the film, or that we wouldn't care [that she didn't adhere to her contract]. She played Russian roulette with her job and her career, and boy, did she lose, *big-time*!"

After months of being out of work, my client found a new job for a substantially lower salary in a new market, in which she had to once again establish herself—a horrible end to this story.

Constructive and self-enhancing Career Choreography demands that you do not take unwarranted risks with your precious career. On the contrary, choreography principles dictate that you take well-thought-out and carefully calculated steps that put the percentages heavily in your favor that you will achieve your long-term *Goals* and live your *Dreams*—and that you *do not* sabotage or severely hinder your career by rationalizing that it's okay to opt for some diminishing immediate gratification.

Always remember:

1. When choosing which career steps to take, always have your *Goals* and *Dreams* squarely in mind, and then take steps that are consistent with your attaining those *Goals* and *Dreams*.

2. Rationalizations and boot-strap arguments that allow you to justify taking steps that will or could jeopardize what you want in the long term are poisonous and career-destructive.

In your career steps and strategies, you must avoid both the appearance of impropriety and gambling with your precious career. Additionally, you must strive to remain above reproach and stay above the fray.

Strata-Gems

1. Someone else's poor behavior is not a justification for you to act poorly or be career-destructive.

2. Be better and smarter than everyone else. Don't sink to another's mediocre levels.

3. DO NOT rationalize away poor, inappropriate, or destructive behavior on your part.

4. DO NOT gamble or play Russian roulette with your precious job or career.

37

PAY ATTENTION TO THE "HOW"

Arrogance kills even the biggest brands.

—COLIN COWHERD

Successful individuals know that it's often not what you do, but how you do it that can determine success. So pay great attention to the "how."

—K.L.

Years ago, NBA megastar LeBron James announced to the world that he had decided to leave his hometown team, the Cleveland Cavaliers, and take his talents to South Beach in order to join the Miami Heat. At that moment, James went from being a hugely admired and beloved icon to one who in a number of circles was criticized.

When you examine the dynamics involved here, it appears that James joined the Heat for very logical and compelling reasons:

1. As one's professional basketball legacy is often determined by how many NBA Championships (or NBA Championship rings) you win, James believed he had a far better chance to capture more of them with the Heat than with the Cavs. As it turned out, this proved to be true, as he won two championship rings with the Heat.

2. He wanted to play alongside fellow superstar and close friend Dwyane Wade, for whom he had tremendous respect.

3. He had great confidence that the Heat ownership/management—especially the brilliant Pat Riley—would make the necessary talent acquisitions and moves to keep the Heat as a viable championship contender year after year. Essentially, James valued the Heat team culture more than that of the Cavaliers.

4. If James won multiple championships with the Heat, his worth and that of his brand could increase exponentially.

Because of these and other valid reasons, James left the Cavaliers when his employment contract expired. Due to the NBA free agency rules, he had every right to make a team change that would bring him huge success and happiness. James even accepted less money from the Heat than he would have earned with the Cavs. Yet, this very understandable decision appears to have struck a negative chord with Cavaliers fans and others.

Why did this happen? From my perspective, the answer lies not in what James did, but in *how* he and/or those who collaborated with him seemingly choreographed "The Decision," which aired on ESPN. What follows are just some of the faux pas that appear to have been made in the ill-conceived "Decision" choreography.

Allegedly, James didn't have a private conversation with Cavs management before letting the world know that he had decided to leave the Cavs and sign with the Heat; purportedly, the Cavs first learned that James was leaving Cleveland along with everyone else, when he announced it on "The Decision" special.

Akron, Ohio, was where James grew up and lived. He was a high-school superstar in the area. Akron was his hometown, and he was considered their son and hero. Because he did not show the appropriate respect to his hometown team and fans by telling them first, James appeared to be insensitive, even if, in reality, this was not the case.

Additionally, Cleveland, along with other Rust Belt cities, has had more than its share of setbacks and challenges. James's apparent poorly choreographed choices and acts seemed to be as rude a slap in the face as anyone could give an already beaten-down region and fan base. It just felt and looked wrong!

Constructive Career Choreography mandates that James should have let the Cleveland Cavaliers and their fans know *first* of his decision to leave Cleveland, along with how much he cherished his experience with the Cavs and their fans. Then, a few days later, after the dust had settled, he could have announced that he would be joining the Heat.

The fact that James made "The Decision" public, on a highly promoted, hourlong ESPN special, again made him appear to be insensitive—especially when he announced that he was abandoning his hometown team. To add insult to injury, the world had to wait until about forty minutes into the special to finally learn what James's decision was. This certainly ratcheted up the negative feelings of some viewers. The fact that all of the money earned on the special would go to the Boys Clubs of Connecticut was lost on most everyone due to the strong, vitriolic emotions that were triggered. As a result, a seemingly highly positive act—giving a large amount of money to an excellent charity—was nowhere as well received as it should have been because of how James delivered his message.

Then, to add fuel to the already seething, emotion-laden fire, a few days later, James, flanked by his Heat teammates, held a nationally televised all-out celebration in which he guaranteed that the Heat wouldn't just win one title, and "not just two titles . . . not just three titles . . ." et cetera. This apparently poorly conceived spectacle tarnished James in many people's eyes. And even though what James predicted/promised in many respects turned out to be correct, his reputation, persona, and image appeared to be damaged.

It is only due to the fact that LeBron James is one of the best basketball players ever, and apparently a top-drawer, truly good and caring, and squeaky-clean person, that he has been able to repair his image—as our society, on many levels, loves a winner—and winning multiple NBA titles is a great deodorant and disinfectant for almost all ills. However, for everyone who isn't the acknowledged very best in the world at what they do, do not let your press, hype, big talk, promises, and the like exceed your production, or you'll be disliked, resented, or even hated, and have a huge target on your back at which all detractors can take aim.

Career Choreography is all about putting yourself in positions to succeed—and not in a position where the whole world is rooting against you and wanting to see you fail.

I cannot count the number of instances when individuals made logical and prudent decisions but failed to act in an appropriate manner in implementing them. Oftentimes, through poor communication or a lack of communication, relationships are destroyed. I so often hear from a client, "I understood their [management's] decision, but it's *how* I heard or didn't hear about it, or *how* it was delivered, that so angers me."

Once again, it's often not the substance of the message that causes rancor and ill will—it's *how* the message was or wasn't delivered.

As an astute Career Choreographer, always pay attention to and intelligently choreograph the means by which you execute the "how." It's an essential element of success.

Strata-Gem

How you do things is often of equal or even more importance than *what* you do. Pay careful attention to the means by which you choreograph the "how."

38

DON'T BE AN ENERGY VAMPIRE

It is important to be an employee or associate who isn't a constant pain in the butt to deal with. During my years of counseling and coaching, I have seen far too many talented people retard their growth or sabotage their careers by being an "energy vampire." You know, those individuals who always need or cause drama, who constantly demand attention, who continually complain, and who are always negative and cause problems. They just drain you!

I have also seen many individuals whose behavior was so toxic that their companies just let them go, because no matter how talented they were, life's too short to have to put up with needless, distracting, stress-evoking baloney! An illustration of this self-sabotaging dynamic occurred in the case of "Leslie."

Leslie is an actress who had a lucrative and prestigious series role on a popular daytime soap opera. What I have learned about Leslie is that there is something in her background that makes her perceive and feel that everyone is out to "shaft" her. And when Leslie perceives that certain actions taken by others toward her are disrespectful or, as she puts it, "just plain wrong," extremely strong and highly toxic emotions are triggered within her. The predictable result is that Leslie consistently acts out the same self-sabotaging behavioral script of flying into a blinding rage and unthinkingly reacting in a self-destructive manner.

This is exactly what happened when Leslie perceived that her management's offer for a new series contract was a "disgrace" and a clear effort to "shaft" her (her word, not mine). She felt this way despite the fact that her management offered her a token raise during the economically challenging latter half of 2008. Apparently, as soon as Leslie heard management's initial offer, all of her pent-up feelings of pain, hurt, and rejection were triggered and bubbled over. These feelings in turn triggered tremendously potent negative energy charges within her, which led her to make the self-destructive choice to lash out and retaliate against her management by

1. telling her employers that if they didn't give her the kind of raise "she deserves," she wouldn't report to work at the end of the month when her contract expired, and

2. signing a long-term contract with a talent representative with an unsavory reputation, whom she knew her management hated dealing with, simply to spite them.

The catastrophic result was that Leslie's employers withdrew their offer to her and immediately removed her from the show. When the emotional dust settled, and both intellectual clarity and the stark reality set in that she had lost her job and had no other one to go to, Leslie panicked. Her best judgment told her that she'd screwed up . . . in a *big* way. Initially, she asked her new representative to go back to her employers and request that they reinstate their offer and her job. However, her employers were only too happy to tell this representative, whom they detested, "No! It's too late. She should have thought about the repercussions of her acts and threats *before* she drew her line in the sand."

Upon receiving this news, Leslie became even more terrified. She then personally went to management (with her tail between her legs) and begged for her job back—*even if she received no raise.* Unfortunately for Leslie, management had lived through "way too many" of her angry reactions. They told Leslie's representative that they were "over her," as "life's just too short!" As a result, Leslie was told to pack up her things and "be off the lot by the end of the day."

Devastated in every way, Leslie left her job with no other position to go to and with no prospects of future employment during a terrible economic time.

Always remember, it is human nature in business to seek out pleasurable experiences and those with whom we have them, as well as to avoid uncomfortable and painful experiences and those individuals who cause them.

Positive people often have positive career encounters because, at the end of the day, life is too short for negativity. Don't be a drama queen (or king)!

Strata-Gem

Don't be an energy vampire, as you run the risk of employers and associates not wanting you around!

39

YOU WANT THE LEVERAGE IN CONTRACT NEGOTIATIONS

Leverage exists when your employer believes,
That if the deal's not good, you will leave.
Leverage doesn't, in fact, have to be real,
For you to secure a really good deal.
But it's great when you can back up the talk,
That if you're not happy, you will walk!

—K.L.

Years ago, whenever I'd open an airline magazine and see Chester Karrass's advertisement for his negotiation seminars and tapes, I was struck by his quotation (also the title of one of his books): "In business, you don't get what you deserve, you get what you negotiate."

When it comes to most instances in business, I agree with Dr. Karrass. Whether or not you can negotiate a fair, good, or great deal almost always depends upon whether you have the leverage to do so. Leverage consists of (at least) four elements:

1. How much an employer or a prospective employer wants to retain or acquire your services (this is usually the most important element)

2. What the employer perceives your marketability to be or what your ability is to walk away from the deal

3. How much you want or need the deal

4. Whether you are willing to—or actually do—walk away from the employer's final offer

Here are four illustrations of the impact that leverage had upon my negotiations.

....

1. A few years ago, I was negotiating a deal for a well-established business reporter in a top market. The news director with whom I was negotiating said his station would absolutely not pay more than a five-percent annual increase over the reporter's $150,000 salary, for a new three-year contract. When I told him that I wanted in the mid-$200,000 range as a starting point for my client, and that I thought I could get an offer of about $250,000 at a competing station in the market, he cavalierly responded by saying, "Kenny, if she can get that kind of an offer, she should take it. But we're not going to pay more than a five-percent raise. That's it!"

Two days later, I received a three-year offer of $240,000, $250,000, and $260,000 for my client to work at a competing station in the market—an offer that my client would have been more than happy to accept if her current employer didn't appropriately respond. With leverage and confidence in hand, I called the news director at my client's current station to advise him that my client had decided to decline his offer of a five-percent raise. No hard feelings. The news director nervously said that I should not do anything until he called me back. Within ten minutes, I received a call from the station's general manager, who said, in as friendly a manner as possible, "Kenny, my goal in running this station is to have as many [on-air] employees as possible receiving three- to five-percent raises."

I replied, as cavalierly as possible, "We know that, so we're not pushing you to pay any more. My client will just turn in her resignation . . ."

"But," he interrupted, "there are times when we have to and need to keep someone, and we'll do what it takes. You've forced us to pay the market price. Let's get this one over with. We'll pay your client $260,000, $275,000, and $300,000 for a three-year, no-cut [firm] deal."

Because we had leverage, my client received an average of over $100,000 per year more than what the news director had told us his final offer was!

....

2. Another client of mine was offered an anchor position by a prominent network. This client was already a successful, well-paid anchor in his local market, where he was happy to stay. Twice he turned down the network's generous offer, but he finally decided to accept the position only if the network would agree to the almost nowhere-to-be-found termination clause: If my client was unhappy for any reason, he could terminate the contract and work for someone else. When I asked the network negotiator for the clause, he responded that he could *never* give that clause. "No way, no how." I took his reply

back to my client, who was happy to forget the whole thing
. . . which he did. Two weeks later, the network once again
offered him the position, along with an increased compensation package. My client once again said, "No—but thank you."

The next day, the negotiator called and said (in a tone of
half-resignation and half-admiration for my client): "Okay.
Your client can leave at any time—except during a ratings
period—with sixty days' notice, and one caveat: He cannot terminate to go to another network."

Because of the leverage derived from my client's
(repeated) willingness to walk away from the network's
offer, he was able to secure a truly extraordinary deal.

....

3. There is a middle-market station with which I have done a
    great deal of business through the years. Because of the high
    quality of both the station and my clients' work, I have been
    able to take three or four of their on-air people to wonderful
    and prominent positions. Additionally, because of my track
    record, and because of how talented and marketable this sta-
    tion perceived a particular client of mine to be, a year and a
    half into a three-year agreement, the general manager called
    and said, "Kenny, I know you're gonna move your client if
    we don't sign her now [to a new deal], so let's just double her
    salary and cut through the bulls—t."

    I called my client, who had every intention of staying at her
    station for the foreseeable future—as long as she had the right
    contract. After hearing the offer, she told me to get whatever
    else I could, and then accept it. A little later, I called the general
    manager, appropriately improved the deal, and then closed it.
    My client was ecstatic.

    In this instance, my perceived ability to effectively

market my client and her perceived marketability gave us leverage—in spite of the fact that not one prospective employer had even been approached to possibly hire my client (so early in her contract).

....

4. Another client of mine, who was at a network-owned station in market "A," made his wishes known that he really would like and, in fact, needed to be transferred across the country to a station owned by the same network in market "B." The market "B" station was willing to find a spot for him, but they could basically "take him or leave him."

When it came to his moving expenses, they stayed firm at $3,500 to move all of his belongings cross-country. He secured three moving estimates, the lowest of which came in at $4,500. When I learned that my client would have to go out-of-pocket to move to his desired station, I called to reason with the news director of station "B," hoping he would authorize payment of my client's moving expenses. I began the conversation (with some tongue-in-cheek humor): "My client just got three moving estimates, and the lowest one is $1,000 more than your extraordinarily generous offer of $3,500. So why don't you cover his total expenses (of $4,500), we'll call it a day, and you can feel good about yourself on your deathbed?"

"Nope. $3,500. That's it," the news director replied.

I responded, in my most humane tone, "But 'Steve,' three months ago, you gave me $30,000 as a moving allowance for my other client to move from her home two hours away. Be fair!"

He replied, with what he perceived as perfect logic, "We *really* wanted your other client, and by giving her all that money for moving, she was able to put more in her pocket, because we couldn't pay her all that you asked for in salary. In this client's case, *he* wants to move here, and so far as we're concerned, we're happy to have him, but we'll live if we don't. The 'deathbed' stuff was a good effort, but sorry, $3,500. That's it!"

....

The moral of these stories is: *You* want the leverage when you negotiate your employment agreements.

Strata-Gems

1. Leverage can enable you to negotiate and secure more advantageous assignments, security, salary, or benefits.

2. There are at least four elements of leverage:

   a. How much an employer or a prospective employer wants to retain or acquire your services

   b. What the employer perceives your marketability to be or what your ability is to walk away from the proposed deal

   c. How much you want or need the deal

   d. Whether you are willing to—or actually do—walk away from the employer's final offer

3. *You* always want the leverage!

DO NOT LEAVE YOUR JOB BEFORE SECURING AN ENHANCING POSITION ELSEWHERE

As businesses change, individuals often find their workplaces are no longer as desirable or beneficial as they once were, or they feel they need to leave in order to grow.

When someone first hires you, they are excited about you, and they believe that you are *the* answer—or at least *an* answer—to their problems or needs, and they look to use your services as much as possible. However, when management, research, goals, or perceptions change and you are no longer coveted, or at the top of management's list, these changes have the potential to profoundly affect you, professionally and psychologically. When you work for someone who doesn't see your talent, doesn't believe in you, or doesn't treat you well, you can easily lose self-esteem and confidence. It's like being in a bad or abusive relationship. You can begin to think that everything is your fault and that you are not much good at anything or to anyone.

Another reason for making a job change is that regardless of how management feels about you, you perceive that you are no longer growing and challenged, or there is no longer much compelling you to stay.

For these and other valid reasons, you may want or need to move on to a new and healthier position and venue. One rule I always share with my clients is this: If at all possible, do not leave your present position until you have secured another one to go to.

I say this for a number of reasons. First of all, when you are out of work and looking, you are almost always on the defensive. People ask, "Why aren't you still in your prior position?" and "Why didn't it work out?"—as if the departure from your job was your fault. Because of this, you can lose some or a great deal of leverage regarding your next salary, as employers often assume desperation. For example, if your annual salary is $100,000 and you leave your job, you are now earning *nothing*. On the other hand, I have found that if you are still earning $100,000, when you negotiate a salary with a new employer and that employer asks what you are currently earning, they will likely do one of three things:

1. Offer you a raise

2. Match your current salary

3. Offer you a bit less because of the financial exigencies of the economy or the state of the company's finances

However, if you are earning nothing, the employer will not feel at all compelled to offer you a raise or match your prior salary. It is far more likely that with no current salary for you to bargain with and use as an all-important base negotiating figure, you may well be offered a substantial pay cut.

Additionally, if you had any real discord or problems at your last job that you would rather a prospective employer not hear about, then

I would definitely advise you to stay at your current position until you have found a new one. I recommend this because a prospective employer will most likely not consult with your current management about you while you are still at your current job, but *will* ask questions of your previous employer.

A memorable example of this occurred when a very bright news director had a bitter falling-out with her new general manager. As a result of this dispute, the news director quit her job, even though she had no new position to go to. Thereafter, when she interviewed for potential positions that she was more than qualified for, she wasn't hired. Eventually she was forced to resurrect her career by accepting a relatively low-paying position at a station in a much smaller market than the one she left. At some point, she learned why she had been shut out from the better positions that she should have secured: Her former general manager, with whom she had the squabble, essentially sabotaged her chances when potential employers called him to do a reference check. Allegedly this general manager didn't actually say bad things about the applicant, but he was able to nix the former news director's chances of securing work by what he *didn't* say.

My advice is that you keep your friends close, and keep working for your potential enemies until you have secured your next job.

Of course, there may come a time when your self-esteem is so low, or when you are so unhappy and feel so underutilized and unwanted, that you just do not want to endure any more anguish and humiliation. In this case, it may be healthier for you to leave. However, this should be a last resort.

Strata-Gems

1. It's ideal to stay at a position until you have an enhancing position to go to. Conversely, there are times when you are so dissatisfied or demoralized that your emotional and physical health must be preserved at all costs. In that case, it may be wise to leave a position *before* you secure another one. Be sure to explore all possible options and consequences before you make this move.

2. Keep working for your potential detractors or enemies until you have found and locked in your next job or position. To help yourself get through this uncomfortable period, try to remember, it's just temporary!

41

TAKE THE CONSTRUCTIVE HIGH ROAD WHEN LEAVING YOUR CURRENT JOB

The other day, a client called to tell me that he had just spoken with his management, and they had advised him that the option in his contract for him to be renewed for two more years was not going to be exercised. As a result, in sixty days, he would be out of work. My client then proceeded to complain about how the managers who hired him had all been replaced, and that the new executives had never taken the time to explain their vision of and expectations for what they wanted from him. So, he was left to navigate things in the dark.

As my client spoke, you could hear his bitterness. After he finished venting, I counseled him that even though everything he said was correct, he needed to take the initiative to leave his firm and all the key players there with positive feelings about him and his experience at the company. Taking these actions is essential for at least two reasons:

1. As we discussed in the previous chapter, once you are out of work, prospective employers will call your last employer to learn what they can about you, including your work habits and your character. By leaving things on a positive, gracious, and appreciative note, you put the percentages in your favor that a past employer will say or imply positive things about you—or at least that they will not go out of their way to hurt you.

2. It's a small world. You never know when your paths with your current employers may cross again—so leave them feeling good and positive about you.

Strata-Gem

Whenever you leave a job or position, leave on a positive, appreciative, and gracious note. It can only serve you well in the future.

42

CHOREOGRAPHIES CAN GO AWRY AND MAY NEED MODIFICATION

Man makes plans, and God laughs.

—UNKNOWN

When circumstances change, great Choreographers constructively adapt by making beneficial adjustments to their Choreographies.

—K.L.

As you've gleaned, this book is devoted to carefully planning the most logical, success-evoking job or career steps. Oftentimes, however, unexpected occurrences come your way. As a result, all bets are off, and your best-crafted choreographies need to be shelved or at least modified. In fact, some of the biggest and most impactful career moves that I've made wound up being totally unplanned and non-choreographed.

For example, when I graduated from law school, I envisioned

myself practicing entertainment or sports-contract law. But just as I was about to be offered a position as an attorney in the entertainment division of a New York City law firm, I learned that one of its major clients was the world-renowned William Morris Agency. This was certainly positive information, as the agency's president was my dad's childhood best friend, Sam Weisbord. I decided to take a trip to California and meet with Sam. My explicit goal was to establish a relationship with the president of my soon-to-be employer's biggest entertainment client. What unexpectedly evolved from that meeting was Sam convincing me that I didn't want to work for the law firm, but rather, that I should work for William Morris. His choreography would be for me to begin as a business-affairs attorney and learn to be an agent through a course of training that would be carefully crafted for me.

After Sam glowingly told me about all of the exceedingly talented and creative individuals whom William Morris represented, I decided that evening to forgo the lucrative offer that was about to be extended to me by the law firm, to instead work for William Morris for less than half the salary the law firm would offer me. This turned out to be a brilliant decision, as the joy and intellectual stimulation that I experienced working for the New York City William Morris office was incredible.

That was unexpected career-course change number one.

During my stint as a business-affairs attorney for William Morris, I realized that one of my strengths was identifying talented individuals and bringing them to the agency for representation. As a result, I'd arrive at the office at 7:30 in the morning (the office officially opened at 9:30), in order to complete my business-affairs contract work early in the day, so I could then focus on contacting and speaking with potential clients in the acting, producing, and music areas. As time passed, I continued to bring more and more valuable clients to William Morris. Then, one Sunday, I was playing in a pro/celebrity tennis tournament, and I met an exceedingly talented, charismatic, bright young news anchor from the local New York City ABC station, Ernie Anastos. After the tournament, Ernie and I chatted, and I explained that I perceived him to have great potential as a national morning-show host. Apparently, Ernie shared my vision of his career track, as the next day, he called to tell me that he would like me to represent him. I explained that while I wasn't an agent, I would be more than happy to arrange for him to meet the head of our news department, Jim Griffin.

As fate would have it, during the two days between Ernie's call to me and his meeting at William Morris, two agents who were working in the news department left the agency. As a direct result, Lee Stevens, the head of the New York office, strongly recommended that I become a news agent—a career course that up until that point had never crossed my mind. After some lengthy discussions with Lee and others, I decided to become an agent in the news department.

That was unexpected career-course change number two.

About seven years later, with my having moved to Los Angeles to be the vice president in charge of news for the William Morris Beverly Hills office, some of the executives there just didn't see the (great) value of having a top-notch news and hosting department in that office. They also made it clear that they didn't want me "wasting my time" developing up-and-coming news talent, as these execs deemed this pursuit as cost-ineffective for the agency, given their substantial overhead expenses. So they repeatedly talked to me about leaving news representation and going into a more mainstream area, such as being a television or motion-picture talent agent. When I resisted following their suggestions, they moved me across the street—away from the other television agents—to an office in the accounting department.

By that time, I had grown to love newscaster and host representation, and I believed these areas were going to materially grow in the upcoming years. This recognition, coupled with my banishment to an isolated office across the street, made me consider what I had never before thought about: Instead of being a William Morris "lifer," I would leave William Morris and open up my own news and hosting agency—Ken Lindner & Associates, Inc.—which I soon accomplished.

Fortunately, almost all of my William Morris clients left to join me after I started my own firm, and many more came to our firm thereafter. Today, more than thirty years later, my representation firm is arguably the most successful and well-respected news and hosting agency in the country.

Through my company, I can offer a more competitive commission structure than most of the major theatrical agencies, and from my vantage point, give clients better representation. I can also continue to pursue one of my passions, which is to develop up-and-coming talent. Because I run my own company and dictate the course of my career, my job security isn't in the hands of a board of directors (please see what happened to Ted Turner when he sold CNN).

In addition, my job enjoyment and satisfaction have increased exponentially since I've had my own firm. I say this to let you know that you can find creative, exhilarating life fulfillment and success away from big companies and "Big Brother" when your original choreographies go awry or need to be modified.

Leaving William Morris and forming Ken Lindner & Associates was my unexpected career-course change number three.

These three stories illustrate that even when you're implementing the most structured and seemingly foolproof choreographies, career doors will unexpectedly open and close. The key, as we will discuss in the next chapter, is to be open, flexible, adaptable, and creative when you need to make major choreography detours and amendments. But please understand that even though unexpected events occurred, and I had to rework some major choreography steps along the way, throughout the years, I have crafted many thousands of choreographies that have gone without major change and have been wildly successful.

Strata-Gem

As an astute and success-evoking Career Choreographer, be aware that in a number of instances, unanticipated life or professional events will occur that may call for you to modify choreography steps, and in some instances, create a whole new choreography in order for you to attain optimal success.

43

BE FLEXIBLE, ADAPTABLE, AND CONSTRUCTIVE

If you're flexible,
you'll never be bent out of shape!

—DEB MAYWORM, former president
and treasurer, Women of Reform Judaism,
Southwest District

As we discussed in the preceding chapter, not every choreography you craft will go as planned. As a result, you must be able to productively and fluidly adapt to changes and unexpected events.

Flexibility and adaptability are essential to attaining and enjoying consistent and sustained success. You can be the most brilliant *choreographer*, but if you can't constructively react to unexpected or undesirable changes, you will be less likely to be fruitful in your endeavors. As the wise national sports radio host Colin Cowherd said about a prominent pro quarterback who appeared to no longer want to learn and grow, "If you're not adaptable, you're not viable."

Great hitters in baseball say that they are mentally relaxed at the plate and hit the ball wherever it's pitched. Similarly, consistently successful individuals are able to be flexible, adaptable, and constructive when confronted with roadblocks or bumps. And, although few individuals relish dealing with problems, truly successful people know that having to work unexpected challenges to their advantage is part of the *Goal*-attainment process. In essence: It's something you gotta do, so do it as effectively as you can.

My dad loved solving problems. He said that challenges made him better, and being flexible is "what positively separated [him] from the 'rigid' executives who didn't fulfill their potential." My dad always taught his trainees to be relaxed when dealing with people or problems, because if you're rigid or uptight, "you'll be less likely to see the Big Picture and find a creative win-win solution. You'll also make everyone else uptight and nervous, and they'll lose confidence in your ability to reach a successful outcome."

Think of it this way: We are all performers in life. And in almost all instances, we will perform better and fulfill our best potential if we are relaxed, open, and having fun—as opposed to being rigid or anxious.

Makes sense, right?

As a skilled choreographer, you will always have your blueprint of the steps you would ideally like to take in order to achieve your *Goals* and *Dreams*. But your best-laid game plans can often go astray. When an unexpected or problematic curve or obstacle is thrown your way, you must be flexible and meet that curve in such a way that you not only hit it—but hit it out of the park!

An invaluable success-evoking asset for you is to learn to perceive every unexpected event, challenge, or obstacle as a golden opportunity to make something good or great happen. We all know the cliché "When you're handed lemons, make lemonade." Let me give you an illustration of this dynamic, and what being constructive is and how it can positively impact what appears to be a disastrous turn of events.

"Bill" is an exceedingly talented anchor and reporter who, like many of my clients, moved from market to market, learning, growing, enhancing his skills and experiences, and working toward increasing his salary in the process. One of the downsides to living this nomadic lifestyle is that it can be upsetting and unsettling to spouses and children who have to uproot and leave friends whenever another market move needs to be made.

After enduring a number of moves, Bill was given the position of main weeknight anchor for a Phoenix television station. According to Bill, this was the first time during his career and in his marriage that everyone in his family was happy. Bill loved his job, and his family loved the city they were living in. All was blissful . . . until Bill's news manager was fired, and he was replaced by "Cal." Soon after Cal took over, he called to tell me that he was sorry, but at the end of the week, Bill would be taken off his prestigious weeknight-evening anchor shift and would instead anchor the weekday-morning newscasts. As Bill was a late-night person, I knew that having to get up at two a.m., five days a week, would make him sick to his stomach. To make matters worse, in two months, when Bill's contract cycle ended, his pay would be cut by fifty percent. The final blow was that at some undetermined point in the future, Bill would be relieved of his anchoring duties altogether.

For Bill, this would be a huge career blow, an economic blow, a confidence blow, and a very public humiliation. So before calling him, I needed to gather my big-picture thoughts and choreography as to how we could both make this turn of events as constructive a situation as possible.

I then called Bill to tell him the seemingly horrible news. As expected, he was devastated for both himself and his family. I tried to console him by explaining that in my many years of experience, I've gleaned that things do happen for a reason, but we don't always immediately see what that reason is. The optimal thing to do, I suggested, was for him to remain constructive during this most trying and demoralizing time.

After a moment or two of thought, Bill replied, "But what does being constructive mean in my case?" Anticipating that Bill would ask me this question, I had already given Bill's situation considerable thought before I called him. As a result, I was quick and confident in my response, saying, "Bill, there are three things you can do now:

1. Remain professional, take the high road, and act as if nothing's happened. No pity parties here. Remember, no one can hurt you unless *you* let them!

2. Anchor the next three weeknight newscasts with passion and purpose! In fact, be the very best that you can be—show the station management that they're making a huge mistake.

3. Come Monday, you will be anchoring the morning newscasts. Let's look at the positive component of this new assignment. These morning newscasts will allow you to show much more of your warm personality, your great sense of humor, your ability to ad-lib, and your ability to conduct great interviews. I look at this as an amazing opportunity to show sides of you that my current anchoring demo tape could never show, because your evening newscasts are so serious and tightly packed." I went on to tell Bill that "being assigned to anchor mornings is a brand-spanking-new, fresh canvas for you to paint on. Do your best to decompress over the weekend. Take your family out to a great dinner. My treat! And then go in Monday morning, show 'em your stuff, and make each morning a masterpiece painting. Go get 'em, Rembrandt!"

As best as he could, Bill understood that anchoring mornings would give him an opportunity to show much more of his likable personality. He agreed to do his best, although he was profoundly hurt and growing angrier by the minute with the apparent snap decision made by his new manager.

Starting the following Monday, Bill did show his stuff. Many station managers were surprised by how he lit it up in the mornings. Within two weeks, Cal called to say that he was seriously rethinking taking Bill off mornings. I was relieved and thrilled.

Then about a week later, the general manager of a top-rated station in Los Angeles visited the Phoenix area and watched Bill anchor throughout the week. He called me to say that in all of the years I had been sending Bill's demo tapes to him, he never saw Bill's charismatic and warm personality, to which I had always attested. He went on to say he was convinced that Bill would make a great anchor for his five p.m. newscast and asked if Bill was contractually available. I told him that Bill's change of anchor assignments triggered an escape clause in Bill's employment agreement. Therefore, he could accept an offer if the deal made sense.

The general manager tendered an offer the next day that was almost too good to be true. Bill accepted it because it was a great career step for him and because it made his wife happy, as her family lived in the Los Angeles area, and because this was a station in a city he could envision working and living in for the rest of his career. So, his children wouldn't have to be uprooted yet again.

The moral of this happy-ending story is that life can certainly throw you curves, and the most well-conceived choreographies might need to be altered. The keys to securing a positive and successful outcome are as follows:

1. Commit yourself, even when you are disheartened, to being as *constructive* and *adaptable* as possible under any and all circumstances.

2. Trust that during challenging times, if you do the right and highly constructive things, good things will happen (my "Just Trust Rule").

3. Creatively figure out what being constructive means and entails in the situation you're dealing with.

4. Effectively implement your constructive steps.

Here is another example of being constructive. My client Dayna Devon was working in Memphis, anchoring her station's week-night newscasts. From the time I started representing Dayna, her *Dream* was to host a national entertainment-news show, such as *Extra*, *Entertainment Tonight*, or *Access Hollywood*.

One day, I received a call from a news executive of a Houston station, who wanted to fly Dayna in for an interview and audition. Dayna was excited about the opportunity because she was eager to grow and at the same time be geographically closer to her family, who lived in San Antonio. I was less enthusiastic about it, as I didn't see it as the right next career step for her, because I felt that she could, in the near future, do better.

The audition and interview at the Houston station didn't go well. Dayna, being relatively young, had little experience with the auditioning process and came off as a bit green and unpolished. By the time she finished her meetings and was on her way to the air-port, I had already spoken to the news manager of the station that auditioned her, who told me that Dayna had great potential but was not quite ready for the job.

When Dayna arrived at the airport, she called to tell me how poorly the meetings and audition had gone. The station managers had asked her in-depth questions about Houston, as well as about the station's parent company, and she hadn't anticipated these subjects as interview topics.

When I told her she was not going to get the job, she was devastated. I felt terrible for her but counseled her by saying that things happen for a reason and that she was not supposed to get *that* job—she was supposed to learn from the experience, so when the right position for her did become available, she would nail both the audition and the interview. I continued, "Just learn from this and stay constructive."

A couple of days later, when the sting of the disappointment began to dissipate, Dayna called me and said, "Okay, let's go over what I did wrong so that it never happens again"—a highly constructive decision on Dayna's part, and we did exactly that.

About six months later, a weekend anchor position on *Extra* became available. Despite the concerns of the show's executive producer that my client was too young and inexperienced for the job, he trusted me that Dayna was indeed ready to shine in the position and flew her to Los Angeles for an interview and audition. She arrived in L.A. the day before the interview so she would be well rested and relaxed for the next day's meetings—another constructive decision. We had dinner that night, and I was greatly encouraged by how well prepared she was. She knew everything about the history of the show, its executive producer, and the company that produced it. She had also taped ten days' worth of shows and had carefully studied the anchor's delivery and body language, as well as *Extra*'s content.

Dayna's interviews and audition went smashingly! After about three months of waiting, she was offered *Extra*'s weekend anchor position. When I told Dayna the good news, she cried with happiness. I was thrilled beyond belief for her, because she is a top-flight, highly talented professional who had turned what initially seemed like defeat into a constructive learning experience.

After she calmed down, I reinforced my perspective by telling her, "See, things *do* happen for a reason. You weren't supposed to get that Houston job. You were meant to have that interview experience *and learn from it*—and you did. I'm thrilled for you, but even more important, I respect and admire you."

Approximately three and a half years later, Dayna was promoted to her ultimate *Dream* position—the main host of *Extra*.

Strata-Gems

1. In your career, as in life, you are dealt certain hands, some advantageous, some extremely challenging. Stay constructive when you suffer what appears to be a major bump in the road. If you can find the most constructive means to weather a career storm or a choreography detour, the results will often be unexpected growth, success, and happiness.

2. Things in life often happen for a reason. Go with the flow and stay calm—this way, you can make the most career-enhancing moves without your decision-making processes and judgment being clouded by the sabotaging emotions of fear, anger, or resentment.

44

"EUM"—EMOTION AND URGE MANAGEMENT[13]

We let our emotions take over our lives every day.

—COLIN COWHERD

It can take twenty years to build a reputation,
and five minutes to destroy it.

—WARREN BUFFETT

Focus on and deal with what you can control,
not what you can't. You can control your thoughts,
your emotions, your choices, and your actions.
Successful individuals know how to control their emotions;
they don't let their emotions control or sabotage them.

—K.L.

---

13   The topic of mastering your emotions, urges, and impulses is the subject of my book
Your Killer Emotions: The 7 Steps to Mastering the Toxic Emotions, Urges, and Impulses
That Sabotage You.

O ftentimes, we know what our *Goals* and *Dreams* are, and what steps we need to take in order to realize them. We're also cognizant that we must be disciplined at appropriate times so we don't opt for an immediately gratifying, but ultimately less-satisfying, quick fix in lieu of striving to attain our most cherished *Goals* and *Dreams*.

Intellectually, we *know* all of this. But when we're flooded with anger or rage, or feelings of hurt, rejection, disrespect, hopelessness, jealousy, resentment, and the like—or urges that are sexual or competitive in nature—these emotions often override and dismantle our sound reasoning processes, and as a result we make self-destructive and career-sabotaging decisions.

Let me share three stories with you.

....

1. A talented young man named "Terrell" worked for a coffee franchise's local shop. His *Goal* was to become a manager of one of the chain's stores, while his *Dream* was to own three or four of them. As an employee, Terrell was both conscientious and cordial to the customers. However, Terrell also demonstrated some significant behavioral issues that needed to be addressed. One of Terrell's problems was that he didn't suffer fools easily, and the manager of his store was clearly a slacker. Second, Terrell had a flash temper—especially when he felt he was being disrespected.

    During his year of working at the coffee shop, he brought a number of things that needed to be remedied or fixed to his store manager's attention. The manager, who viewed Terrell as a threat to one day take his job, paid little or no attention to Terrell or to the problems that he identified. This infuriated Terrell for two reasons: First, Terrell took great pride in his work and in the shop itself; second, Terrell felt disrespected by his manager, who seemed to enjoy angering the much more engaging and popular Terrell.

One night, one of the shop's outdoor tables that was screwed into the concrete was vandalized. The next morning, all that remained was the protruding, screwed-in metal base, which posed a clear hazard to customers who could easily trip over it. Twice Terrell told his manager that the manager needed to put some sort of visible warning sign around the base in order to avoid potential customer or staff-member injury. Both times the manager ignored him.

About fifteen minutes later, a customer tripped over the base and spilled his coffee all over his shoes and pants. Luckily, the patron kept his balance, so he wasn't hurt. When the customer came into the shop to report the incident, Terrell exploded like a lit powder keg, as he said in a voice loud enough for everyone, including his manager (who was busy placating the unhappy customer), to hear: "I told our ignorant manager about what would happen. But he didn't pay any attention to me. He looks at me like I'm a fool. But the only fool here is him! A lazy, fat fool at that! S**t, I told him twice to fix that thing!"

The manager, realizing that he could lose his job over this incident, apologized to the customer and gave him a twenty-five-dollar gift card along with a new drink. And as soon as the customer left, the manager fired Terrell for "behavior unbecoming of an employee of the company" and for his "public use of foul language."

A few moments later, the sad reality sank in: Terrell realized that he gave his manager all of the ammunition he needed to derail the career that Terrell dearly treasured with his company. Alas, Terrell working for—much less owning—any of his former employer's shops was no longer a possibility.

....

2. "Brandon," thirty-six, was an accountant for a top-eight firm. He was married with two children and had been with his firm for seven years. "Janna," twenty-four, was a recently hired assistant at the firm. She was married with no children.

It was common knowledge at the firm that office romances and affairs were strongly frowned upon by the board of directors. However, one sultry Thursday evening, at a company retreat, Brandon and Janna hooked up for a torrid night of sex. Brandon engaged in this behavior *fully aware* that he was under serious consideration to be made a firm partner.

Somehow Janna's husband found out about the one-nighter and, in a rage, called Brandon's wife and some of the company's board members. As a result of the situation becoming public and uncomfortable for everyone at the firm, Brandon was not made partner. Soon thereafter, he was told to leave the firm. At the same time, Brandon's wife filed for divorce and sought sole custody of their children. He never saw Janna again.

At the end of the day (or evening, as it were), Brandon was left with nothing. A few days after leaving his firm, with intellectual clarity restored, he realized how he had totally ruined his life—for a mere one-night affair.

....

3. Years ago, Ron Artest, a star professional basketball player for the NBA's Indiana Pacers, was waiting to reenter a game against the home-team Detroit Pistons.

Suddenly, Artest was hit and drenched with a cup of beer, which was thrown at him by a Detroit fan. Furious, Artest stormed into the stands to retaliate against his assailant. In an enraged instant, he allegedly punched a fan. Immediately, some of Artest's teammates also ran into the stands, at which point violence, and one of the ugliest altercations ever to take place at a sporting event in the United States, quickly ensued.

In the end, Artest was suspended for the rest of the NBA season. The teammates who followed Artest into the stands were also suspended for varying amounts of time.

In mere moments, the following negative chain of events occurred: Artest was pelted with beer and, in a fit of rage, he and his teammates unthinkingly and violently reacted; allegedly, Artest lost millions of dollars in salary, as well as the ability to play for the remainder of the season; and the Pacers' realistic hopes of becoming the NBA champions that season were destroyed.[14]

....

I cannot recount how many times I've seen or heard of talented individuals, who had so many good things going for them, sabotage themselves and their careers by letting their emotions and urges momentarily cloud their better judgment! The profound problem is that one sabotaging moment can destroy a career for years, and possibly a lifetime. This brings us to our final principle.

---

14   Ken Haddad, "15 Years Later: Remembering the 2004 Pistons-Pacers Brawl," Click on Detroit, November 19, 2019, https://www.clickondetroit.com/sports/2019/11/19/15-years-later-remembering-the-2004-pistons-pacers-brawl/.

> Career Choreography Principle 4:
> Never make career decisions or act if your best judgment
> is clouded or dismantled by sabotaging emotions,
> impulses, or urges.

Literally every day I counsel clients on how to deal with *EUM—Emotion and Urge Management*. The way to do this—and the means by which you can stay true to your *Goal-*Attainment Choreography—is through the *7-Step EUM Process*. Here are your career-preserving steps.

Step 1. Do *not* make a decision when you are enveloped and hijacked by toxic emotions and urges. Stop and cool down. Step away from the heat, angst, and seemingly compelling needs of the moment, and wait until calm and intellectual clarity return.

Step 2. *Visualize* your *Big-Picture Goals* and *Dreams*, and how much you want to attain and fulfill them, respectively.

Step 3. *Consider* the most severe and heinous career consequences that could occur if you act out of rage, hurt, rejection, or sexual urge—that is, be consequence cognizant.

Step 4. *Visualize* the negative or even tragic effects that your impulsive acts could have on you, your loved ones, your clients, or anyone and anything that matters to you. Be profoundly aware that just one egregious misstep can negate all of the positive things you've already accomplished in your life! Fatal errors in your career life can and will affect your personal life.

Step 5. *Frame* the issue before you in such an impactful way that you are inevitably compelled to make a career-enhancing choice. The following are examples of *frames* that the three above-mentioned individuals could have constructed in order to avoid sabotaging their careers.

1. Terrell: "My ultimate *Dream* is to be a franchise owner of this company's coffee shops . . . not to be on the street and out of work! So no matter how awful my store manager is, I'm *not* going to let that loser's bad behavior preclude me from fulfilling my *Dream*! Saying out loud what I think of him isn't worth it! It will only be hugely damaging to me.

   "If he won't take care of our shop so that it's clean and safe for our customers and staff, I'll just cool down and wait until I can approach some other person in management who can remedy the situation."

2. Brandon: "As attracted as I am to Janna, I'd be a self-sabotaging idiot to risk my career, my income, my marriage, and my family for an hour in the sack—with her or anyone!

   "So, no matter how much it seems like fun to have a fling with Janna—or any 'Janna'—it's not worth risking all that I have and can attain! I will *not* be self-sabotaging! No Janna for me!"

3. Ron Artest: "I am so freaking angry that this stupid ignoramus Piston fan hit me with a beer. But I'm *not* willing to risk our season, my career, my freedom, my salary, my endorsements, and my image/legacy just to punch this moron! No way! He and the momentary gratification aren't worth it! Instead, I'm going to be smart. I'll get someone from security to arrest this guy, and tomorrow, I'll press charges against him. A much better solution! I'll nail him in court—not off the court!"

Step 6. Do not opt for an act of immediate gratification if it could—in any way—be destructive to you, your career, your loved ones, and/or others.

Step 7. Instead, take as much time as you need to figure out a plan of action (which could mean ultimately refraining from taking any action) that is consistent with—and will facilitate—the attainment of your *Goals* and *Dreams*.

To illustrate the *7-Step EUM Process*, let me share the following personal story.

A number of years ago, I realized that in order for my news and hosting representation firm to continue to evolve and flourish, I wanted to enter into a strategic alliance with a major theatrical agency, so that our two agencies could offer the very finest news, hosting, commercial, acting, digital, speaking, and literary representation to our clients, along with broadcast representation. By entering into the alliance, I perceived that—

1. We could better serve and meet the needs of our current clients.

2. We could secure the representation of clients who needed multi-platform representation—not just broadcasting representation.

3. My staff and I would learn and thereby grow by being exposed to valuable information in various areas.

4. We would develop new and highly lucrative, diverse revenue streams.

As I contemplated achieving all of these significant benefits, I completed negotiations to align with what I deemed to be the best theatrical agency to accomplish our *Goals*. However, just before I received the contract, I was told by one of the agency's top executives—who, I had heard, had a penchant for reneging on important deal points—that one of the key provisions that I had specifically negotiated into our deal had been altered. As soon as I heard about the modification—which was hugely detrimental to our company—my blood began to boil. I so very much wanted to blurt out what an unethical individual I believed him to be for brazenly changing and reneging on our agreement. But I didn't. Instead, I followed the *7-Step EUM Process*:

Step 1. I didn't make a decision or act when I was consumed with anger. Instead, I stepped away from the heat of the moment, to wait until I was calm and I could think, value, and reason clearly.

Step 2. I did my valuation during this process and identified what I wanted most out of the interaction, which was to better serve our clients, expand the range of services we could offer them, and enhance our client list. Therefore, I still wanted to align with the theatrical agency.

Step 3. I considered the toxic consequences of my saying what I thought and felt about the executive's apparent inappropriate behavior.

Step 4. I visualized losing the deal and not reaping the huge benefits of the alliance.

Step 5. I *framed* the issue before me: "Do I want the momentary satisfaction of telling this guy what I truly think of his behavior, or do I want to calm down and figure out a more constructive means of handling the situation and thereby securing a positive, beneficial solution?" By framing the issue in this manner, I realized it was far wiser to hold my tongue and thereby secure what I dearly wanted for our clients and my agency.

Step 6. Framing the issue enabled me to realize that the quick-fix option of retaliation would have blown the deal.

Step 7. I figured out a constructive and creative solution to the problem so that both parties were able to feel as if they'd secured what they needed.

As a result, our two agencies aligned, and both parties enjoyed tremendous success. Unquestionably, the alliance was a huge boon to our business, and to this day, I'm thrilled that I followed the 7-Step EUM Process.

Using the 7-Step EUM Process has enabled and empowered innumerable individuals to make huge-success-evoking career decisions, as opposed to ones that are career-destructive.

THE "COMPETITIVE URGE"

We live in a dog-eat-dog world. We applaud and positively reinforce winners, and unfortunately, we kick also-rans to the curb like yesterday's garbage. This reality puts tremendous pressure on individuals to keep pushing the proverbial envelope in an effort to outdo others.

The problem is that in our efforts to make the sale, get the interview, earn the bonus, or lead the league in home runs, we sometimes engage in behavior that puts the very career that we cherish in great jeopardy. As a Career Choreographer for more than thirty-five years, I've seen greed, egos, character flaws, and competitive urges get the best of individuals as they failed to consider the very real risks and consequences of their actions. A substantial number of these thoughtless, reckless, or self-destructive individuals negated all or many of the wonderful things that they had accomplished during their careers. Others irreparably damaged or lost their careers, and some lost their loved ones and their freedom, as the perpetrators ultimately went to jail.

One Career Choreography rule that I always share with my clients is this: Almost nothing is worth risking the career that you've built, so always carefully consider the career consequences of your acts. And if you find that you're in a position to perform or refrain from performing an act that could put your career or reputation in any kind of risk, in almost all instances, it's wise to err on the side of caution. There will be other nondestructive opportunities to do great things. Remember, your career is precious. Don't blow it!

If you could ask the board members of Enron, John Edwards, David Petraeus, or others whether they now wished that they had considered the consequences of their alleged career-altering acts before they committed them, I would think the unanimous answer would be a resounding "Yes! I would love to turn back the hands of time and take back the damage that I've caused and the humiliation that I and others have suffered!"

The key is to preserve your career by managing and mastering your emotions and urges. Do not diminish or destroy your career or your potential by settling for some momentary gratification—no matter how attractive it appears at the time. Remember, one destructive moment can ruin a career for a lifetime!

Strata-Gems

1. It is not uncommon to have your emotions and urges conflict with and overpower your better judgment. When this happens, you run the risk of acting in ways that are detrimental to the attainment of your *Goals* and *Dreams*. Engage in the 7-Step EUM Process discussed above, and don't opt for the quick, destructive fix in these situations. Instead, *choose* to take actions that will enhance your chances of enjoying long-term career success and fulfillment.

2. Always consider the career and personal consequences of your acts! In other words, be consequence cognizant.

3. Identify and keep in mind what your true long-term *Goals* and *Dreams* are, and make choices that reflect and affect them.

45

THE VIRTUES OF LETTING GO AND BEING PATIENT

Career Choreography is about taking control of the things that you *can* control: your choices, your actions, your mindset, your emotions. As you have read, the spirit of self-determinism pervades Career Choreography. That said, in life, no matter how effective your choreography may be, some things just aren't meant to be or aren't meant to happen on your timetable. Sometimes you are destined to experience the unforeseen. This can turn out to be even more beneficial or instructive for you than what you had originally envisioned or planned.

I am a huge proponent of the insight "Everything in its own time." I have found that no matter how well and astutely planned your choreography is, there are times when you must be patient, let go of your expectations, and willingly accept the flow of life. Put another way, life has its own choreography, so there are times to trust in its natural movement. As we all know, there are some things we can't control, and we must make peace with this. This sentiment is eloquently reflected in the prayer "God, grant me the serenity to accept the things I cannot change, the courage to change the things I can, and the wisdom to know the difference." The secular version of this is one in which you adopt these peace-providing qualities. Embracing them will make your life better on so many levels.

The key is to strike a positive balance between making the very most of what you can control and choreograph, and constructively accepting what God, fate, or whatever force you believe in has in store for you.

Robert Iger, the hugely successful and respected former chairman of the Walt Disney Company, once told me that one of the keys to his success has been his ability to "be patient."

What I took away from Bob's insight is that certain things take time to play out or mature, and if you want to secure a successful result, you must be patient and wait until the time is right in order to reap the seeds you've sown. As timing can be everything, and we live in a quick-fix/give-it-to-me-now society, it's important not to lose sight of how being appropriately patient in the right circumstances can pay major career dividends—as they say, quite often it's advantageous to "play the long game."

Strata-Gems

1. Even the best Career Choreographers cannot control everything, especially when life has its own plans for you. In these instances, the most constructive course of action is to let go of your choreography—or at least for the time being keep it in abeyance—go with the flow, and make the most of the unforeseen and (what may initially appear to be) unfavorable events in your life.

2. Have the serenity to accept the things you cannot change, the courage to change the things you can, and the wisdom to know the difference.

3. Sometimes being patient is the wisest choreography strategy.

QUICK TAKES—
MORE SUCCESS-EVOKING
CAREER STRATEGIES

THE BENEFITS OF BEING GREAT
IN ONE COVETED AREA

While I absolutely subscribe to the concept of laying a solid foundation in everything that you do and acknowledge that it's great and success-evoking to be proficient in a myriad of areas, there's no disputing this: If you're great at *one thing* or *have an extraordinary skill* that society truly covets and highly rewards, you can enjoy huge success in many areas.

For example, if you're a great singer/songwriter/performer (e.g., Taylor Swift, Paul McCartney, Kacey Musgraves, Billy Joel, Kelly Clarkson, Elton John), a star athlete (e.g., Michael Jordan, Peyton Manning, Tom Brady, Roger Federer, LeBron James), a leading actor/actress (e.g., Brad Pitt, Angelina Jolie, Jennifer Aniston), or a top TV host (e.g., Oprah Winfrey, Mario Lopez, Ryan Seacrest, Kelly Ripa, Michael Strahan), you can reach tremendous heights in many areas and have many meaningful doors open for you.

What all of the above "stars" have in common is that they are perceived as being relatively "unique," in that a minuscule number of individuals can do what they can do, as well as they can do it. For all intents and purposes, they are nearly *irreplaceable*. This, in great part, is why they can command such huge salaries for their services. These individuals are paid an enormous amount of money because other individuals (e.g., sports-team owners, film producers, record companies, networks, concert promoters, etc.) make *more* money as a result of employing or being in business with these uniquely talented individuals. These exceptionally skilled individuals are huge revenue generators.

In order to attain huge fame and fortune, one's greatness or uniqueness must involve a skill that our society not only covets but also rewards financially. For example, sadly, being one of the best teachers doesn't fall into this category—even though what extraordinary and inspiring educators do is invaluable for our children and our society. This is the case because we choose not to reward this profession monetarily for at least two reasons: (1) We don't view teachers—even great ones—as truly unique, and (2) no one is directly making money off of teachers, so the profit incentive in our society simply doesn't exist.

So, if great fame and fortune are what you desire, develop an extraordinary and unique skill set in an area that society covets and financially rewards.

THE POWER OF YOUR SMILE

My dad, who was a master negotiator, early on counseled me that "You can accomplish so much more with a smile. A warm smile and handshake open doors, break down defenses, and—in basic psychological terms—invite other people in and make them feel more comfortable and at home."

One excellent illustration of how a warm, bright smile can make a world of positive difference is the case of Earvin "Magic" Johnson, the hall-of-fame former NBA superstar. As soon as Magic appeared on the professional scene, he positively engaged people with his beautiful, open, joyful smile. When Magic smiled, all seemed right with the world.

As a basketball player, Magic was sought after and glorified by the press. Since leaving pro basketball as a player, Magic has been a model entrepreneur and leader and, because of his great popularity, could very well run for public office. What stands out among all of his highly effective gifts is his infectious smile. It has been a great table-setter for his huge success and business acumen.

B.F. Skinner, the father of behaviorism, taught that in almost all instances, we want to do things that are positive and enjoyable, and we do our best to avoid those that we find negative, painful, or fear-evoking. It was through positive and negative experiences and reinforcement that Skinner was able to develop behavioral repertoires. Following Skinner's teaching and Magic's behavior, we are all at some point shy, insecure, fearful, and the like. As a result, we will be far more likely to relax, let down our defenses, and want to interact with someone who greets and treats us warmly and openly, and puts us at ease . . . and the easiest means to begin a positive, success-evoking interaction is with a warm, engaging smile. It's powerful stuff!

DRESS FOR SUCCESS

We've all heard the above cliché, and I have consistently found that dressing well, neatly, and appropriately can make a favorable impression that can increase the chances that you will enjoy a successful encounter. Conversely, if you dress inappropriately for a meeting, you may well make an irreparably poor impression that can significantly diminish your chances of securing a successful result.

Dressing appropriately is success-evoking. Dressing inappropriately is inviting failure. How you do or don't prepare, with respect to the effort that you make to dress for success, says a lot about you. When you are well dressed, well groomed, and polished, the people with whom you meet can readily see that you take pride in yourself and your appearance. Your efforts show that you engaged in *effective preparation*. How you represent yourself to a company reflects how, in all likelihood, you will represent yourself on *behalf* of that company.

In our fast-moving society, we have to make quick judgments and snap decisions; as a result, we often rely on first impressions, which amount to a form of profiling. Dressing well and appropriately sends all sorts of success-evoking signals and positive messages to important others.

DO YOUR BEST TO CONTROL THE ENVIRONMENT AND VARIABLES THAT COULD DIMINISH YOUR EFFORTS AND EFFECTIVENESS

In connection with every meeting or transaction that's important to you, you want to put the percentages heavily in your favor that things will go as well as possible.

For example, when you are meeting important people at a restaurant, make sure that you can—and do—make a reservation beforehand and ensure that you will be seated quickly. This way, you and your guests won't be awkwardly waiting around until a table is ready. Also, ask ahead of time for a table in a quiet part of the restaurant so that you can listen to and *connect* with your guests, and they with you.

Through the years, I have selected one or two restaurants at which to do business, for I know these establishments will seat my guests and me immediately at a desirable table and will always provide top-drawer service. These restaurants also serve a wide variety of excellent dishes to satisfy diverse tastes.

I always arrive at the restaurant at least ten minutes early to make sure everything is arranged correctly. Before my guests arrive, I give the waiter or *maître d'* my credit card so there's no question as to who will pay the check. I also like arriving early for all meetings because it gives me the opportunity to freshen up, prepare my thoughts, and take a moment or two to relax before showtime.

There are even some instances—especially breakfast meetings—when I eat something beforehand so that I can focus my total energies on listening respectfully and effectively responding to the person with whom I'm conducting business.

By taking all of the aforementioned steps, I have gained as much control over my meeting environment as possible, thereby putting the percentages in my favor that I will secure a successful result. These anticipatory steps can be taken wherever you meet. Additionally, I have seen and counseled that a by-product of making these preparatory efforts is the transmission of positive signals about how I choose—and, in fact, carry out—my business. In short, effective preparatory behavior has been very success-evoking for me, my clients, and my company.

STAY AHEAD OF THE CURVE AND ASTUTELY ANTICIPATE

Pray as if everything depends on God;
act as if everything depends on you!
—RABBI DAVID WOZNICA

In any business, you always want to bring as much to the table—and thereby be as valuable to everyone with whom you're involved—as possible. One great way to do so is to be so insightful, proactive, and astutely anticipatory in your thinking that you're almost always ahead of the curve. That is, you're able to anticipate trends, openings, problems, and other individuals' expectations and actions, and then figure out how to make the most of this intelligence.

They say you can often predict the future by knowing the past. So, if you want to be a great prognosticator, do your homework.

DON'T WASTE PEOPLE'S TIME

Although it is success-evoking to have an engaging personality and be pleasingly gregarious in your business endeavors, these qualities must be balanced with a recognition that you must respect people's time. I am always cordial and warm in my business conversations with those individuals who employ or could potentially employ my clients. However, I do not stay on the phone with them longer than necessary. As a result, many individuals will call me back promptly because I'm not a time (or an energy) abuser. In fact, a top-ranking executive at Fox told one of my clients that he always takes my calls because I have a great client list, and I get off the phone quickly.

Be sensitive to other people's time restrictions. This recognition can create and facilitate good working relationships.

LEARN HOW TO DEAL WITH MEDIOCRITY AND TO "SUFFER FOOLS" CONSTRUCTIVELY

When you care about the quality of your work product and you take pride in what you do—but others don't—it can be unnerving, anger-evoking, and thereby potentially career growth retarding. However, if you want to maximize your success, do not lose your cool, your reputation, your lane on the fast track, or your big-picture perspective when you have to deal with mediocre individuals or halfhearted efforts. Instead, figure out a constructive and enhancing way to work with or around these uninspired or untalented individuals, secure the desired top-drawer work product and result that you desire, and then move on.

Remember, it's hard to soar with the eagles when you're tethered to turkeys—but soar you must! Just figure out the most expedient and constructive means to do so . . . and stay cool.

RETURN PHONE CALLS AND CORRESPONDENCE PROMPTLY

If you want to build and nurture relationships, return phone calls and other correspondence in a timely, respectful manner. It will pay career dividends.

SMOKING

Most meeting places have prohibitions against smoking. With that said, don't smoke in *any* business setting. Besides the obvious health risks to you, people generally do not want to breathe in secondhand smoke, and some people associate stigmas like weakness or anxiety with smoking that you don't want applied to you.

We all know that smoking kills. Don't let it kill your career success.

ALCOHOL

I was a social drinker; however, I almost never drank in business settings, as I needed to be razor-sharp, at my best, and always in control. I now don't drink at all.

Many years ago, during a family birthday party, I had a glass of wine on an empty stomach. Apparently, I started making some bold and uncharacteristic statements about something or other. As my dad appeared to be concerned about a stance that I was taking, my mom calmed him down by saying, "That's just the alcohol talking."

Always remember, clients may enjoy drinking with their friends, but they want their advisors to be sober and sharp. When in business mode, you—not your martini—must do the talking. Be brilliant—not buzzed. Your sustained success depends on it.

SLEEP

One of the reasons my dad always looked twenty or more years younger than his chronological age was because he took care to get lots of sleep.

I'm sure that as time goes on, studies will continue to confirm that an appropriate amount of sleep can keep you younger-looking, healthier, and cerebrally sharper. We all know how much more on top of the world we feel when we're fresh and alert, and not emotionally "off."

Always remember, you must cherish your physical well-being. Because if you don't take care of the goose who lays the golden eggs, who will? Get your rest.

EXERCISE

Regular exercise can help you stay fit, relaxed, sharp, and healthy. Once again, be cognizant of the reality that if you don't take care of the "goose that lays the golden eggs," there may no longer be a goose or any golden eggs! So, regular exercise is a must. Take care of yourself and treasure your well-being, as you're all you've got!

THE IMPORTANCE OF PROMPT AND APPROPRIATE FOLLOW-UP

After you have an encounter with an important individual, follow up with appropriate and effective communication. Don't drop the ball. Good follow-up sends a positive message about you.

BE GRACIOUS AND THOUGHTFUL TO THOSE WHO ARE KIND AND HELPFUL TO YOU

A while ago, I completed a negotiation for a client with a network executive. After signing her new employment agreement, my client wrote a lovely thank-you letter to that individual citing her sincere appreciation regarding her new deal. Unexpectedly, my client received a promotion just a few months thereafter, which triggered a renegotiation and good-faith increase of her annual salary. When I called that same executive to discuss an appropriate salary increase for my client, the executive told me about my client's kind letter to her and that she was moved by it. That executive then said that very few people take the time to send their appreciation to individuals who are, as she put it, "behind the scenes." She continued by telling me that she received my client's note at a time when she was a bit "down," and that my client's kind words raised her spirits. Because of the great warm feelings engendered by my client's letter, I know that the executive went to bat with her bosses in a major way for my client, so that my client would get the biggest raise possible—which she did!

What you can take away from this story is that, first and foremost, you will be doing the right thing when you communicate your appreciation to those who are good and kind to you, and are supportive of you. Additionally, it never hurts to have everyone on your side who one day may have a hand or a say in your professional fate and growth.

DO WHAT YOU SAY YOU'LL DO

We all have a million and one things on our mind, but if you promise to do something, make sure that you do it! Reliability, credibility, and veracity are all major components of success. Good follow-through counts—big-time!

COMPLETE WHAT YOU START

Many individuals begin projects, but don't have the focus or discipline to finish them. If the project is worth completing and the *Goal* is worth attaining, finish what you start. Seeing things through to completion is soul-satisfying, esteem-raising, and an essential building block of success.

EFFECTIVELY RUNNING YOUR BUSINESS IS IMPORTANT

Through the years, I have seen the most talent-laden law firms, medical practices, hair salons, and dental offices go under simply because the practitioners didn't know how to run a profitable business. Being a talented artist, attorney, accountant, or hairstylist is one skill—being adept at running and growing a healthy business is quite another.

Make sure that you surround yourself with talented others—office managers, legal counsel, business managers, accountants, assistants, and career advisors who can help you make the most of your talents, while you benefit from their talents and expertise. It's also wise to consult with credible and trustworthy colleagues whenever you are in doubt or on the fence regarding a major decision.

One Saturday afternoon, soon after I started my company, a client met me at my new office and saw me putting tapes alphabetically on shelves. That client caringly shared this hugely insightful perspective with me: "Kenny, why are you spending your valuable time putting tapes on shelves? You should be out signing clients and keeping current clients happy. Hire someone for ten dollars an hour to shelve the tapes and do other jobs like that. Delegate and make the most of your time. You're the rainmaker!"

My client was so right. From that day on, I delegated appropriate tasks and assignments to my stellar support staff, so that I could devote my full time to representing my clients and keeping my business running smoothly.

Successful individuals know or learn what information, expertise, or skills they lack and need, and they associate themselves with first-class individuals who can fill these voids. Build a team and culture of all-stars to support and enhance your productivity. Always remember, "Teamwork makes the dream work!"

TASTEFULLY LET YOUR BOSSES AND CLIENTS KNOW THE POSITIVE THINGS YOU'RE DOING FOR THEM

In the real world, equally talented individuals with comparable accomplishments don't necessarily attain the same levels of success. If you are to attain the success that your skills, achievements, and potential warrant, the individuals you work for need to know what you are bringing and can bring to the table.

If there's a tasteful way for you to have your bosses, customers, or clients become more aware of all the beneficial things you're doing for them, it can only increase your chances to attain success. Essentially, be "P.I."—politically intelligent! For example, I know a talent agent who was able to deftly and tastefully let his clients know all of the beneficial things he was doing for them and their careers. They *loved* him for it, sang his praises to countless others, and were intensely loyal to him. I have done my best to emulate this person's highly constructive behavior.

DEVELOP A THICK SKIN

Hatred corrodes the container it's carried in.

—ALAN SIMPSON, former senator

When you're an unsuccessful person or an underdog, few people are threatened by you; as a result, there is rarely a spotlight on you. However, when you are successful, sadly, many people will be resentful of you and what you've attained. Why? Because these insecure people are envious of your lot in life, as they perceive theirs to be unsatisfying by comparison.

It has frequently been said that we like to build up our heroes so we can knock them down. As you attain more success, you become more of a target for knocks and snipes. Always remember, when individuals take unjustified potshots at you, it's much more about them, and their jealousy, than it is about you. Also keep in mind that you can't please or be respected, liked, or loved by everyone . . . so don't waste your valuable energy trying. Not everyone will get, like, or appreciate you or your talents. Just be the best person and professional you are capable of being, be proud of who you are, and let your detractors stew in their bitter, vitriolic juices.

Success breeds resentment and jealousies. It's unfortunate, and part of business and life. Just have a thick skin, and don't let jealous detractors or competitors distract you and thereby get you to take your eyes off the prize, or rob you of your joy. Also, if you receive negative press or are the victim of hurtful gossip, just do your best to stay cool. Be assured that in our attention-impaired world, the press or the gossip-spreaders will quickly find some other victim to write or talk about. In all likelihood, your story will soon become yesterday's news and of much lesser import.

BE TRUE TO YOUR OWN *GOALS* AND *DREAMS*

Throughout my personal life and my counseling career, I have seen individuals who were driven, conflicted, and tormented by hopes and expectations heaped on them by their parents, spouses, peers, and influential others. And sadly, many of these individuals never were able to passionately pursue their own *Dreams* because they yielded to these pressures and tried to fulfill other people's *Goals* for them. Seemingly controlled by the people around them their whole lives, these individuals felt cheated, angry, and bitter about not being able to direct their own trajectory and freely pursue what would make *their* hearts sing.

If there is one strategy that you take away from this book, then this should be it: As you choreograph your career steps, always be true to *your Goals* and *Dreams*. Make moves and take positions that *you* can live with, because it's *you* who ultimately has to live with them.

Jim Bell, the successful and wise former executive producer of the *Today* show, shared this valuable insight that his father instilled in him from a young age: "Always remember who *you* are!" That is, do things that are consistent with *your* character, conscience, passions, and *Dreams*.

DON'T HITCH YOUR CAREER-WAGON TO INDIVIDUALS YOU DON'T RESPECT

You are often judged by the company you keep or with whom you are professionally aligned. If past experiences or your gut tell you that you cannot trust or respect someone, in most instances, do your best to stay as far away from that person as possible. You do not want to be professionally linked to such individuals.

The renowned philosopher Nietzsche said, "Those who fight monsters must be careful lest they become one." I would rework Nietzsche's insight as follows: "Those who work with or align themselves with monsters must be careful lest they become one and/ or become inevitably linked to one!"

Also, be aware that being associated with sketchy or non-reputable individuals can preclude you from being offered career-enhancing opportunities. Or, as they say, always be aware of who you stand next to or with.

The strategy here is to be very discerning when choosing someone with whom you make your career bed!

BE DETAIL-FOCUSED

Just the other day, a new client of mine was given an amended employment agreement from his company to sign. It provided for a new term and increased compensation. What wasn't obvious to the lay eye was that there was a "boilerplate" provision in the new agreement, the wording of which differed ever so slightly from my client's current employment agreement. Per the current agreement, my client had the right to terminate his relationship with his employer, with seventy days prior notice. The change of wording in his new contract negated that all-important right. Luckily, I caught the nuance and its huge ramifications, much to my client's sincere appreciation. We then immediately remedied the situation by changing the wording in his new employment agreement to mirror that in his current agreement.

I believe I developed a deep reservoir of trust and credibility with my new client because I paid attention to detail. Remember, everyone wants to work with someone who is thorough and buttoned-up.

DEVELOP A WINNING CULTURE

One means of developing a winning culture in your company, on your project, or on your team is to put individuals in success-evoking positions, where everyone involved benefits. Certain positions or assignments can take advantage of and showcase an individual's strengths and minimize or negate their weaknesses. Take time to learn what these strengths and weaknesses are, so you can give the right individuals the appropriate assignments. It is also wise to assign individuals to projects or areas about which they are passionate and enthusiastic.

CHOREOGRAPHED SYNERGY AND CHOREOGRAPHED DIVERSITY

I once had an insight-filled and inspiring lunch with Steve Burke, the wise and gracious then-chairman of Comcast—which owns NBC News. This lunch was attended by the heads of the various divisions of Comcast and took place on the Tuesday following the Super Bowl, which aired on NBC. *The Voice*—NBC's prime-time hit—had made a huge season debut following the Super Bowl, and *Smash*, NBC's new musical drama, had made a very encouraging debut the night before. As a result, the conversation at our table was lively, opinionated, and fascinating. I loved listening to the plans and platforms that these NBC News, NBC Sports, and cable executives were discussing.

Steve explained that he purposely arranges these lunches because the synergy, enlightened perspectives, and diverse ideas that come out of getting his best and brightest individuals to interface in a relaxed setting are invaluable to NBC's and Comcast's continued growth.

What I learned that day is that Comcast and NBC make sure that there are sufficient occasions and venues for their most talented executives to talk and exchange ideas. They make great efforts to attain choreographed synergy, where the sum of the thoughts, perspectives, and talents of their executives becomes incrementally or exponentially greater than its parts.

One other thought comes to mind. It has often been said that individuals like to associate with others who are like them and see things as they do. As the astute, nationally syndicated radio host Colin Cowherd observed, "Often people seek affirmation, not information." This is especially the case if that information conflicts with what these (insecure or defensive) individuals believe and want to hear.

The inherent danger of surrounding yourself with those who think and perceive things as you do is that your ideas and processes are rarely challenged. Better, different, and more situationally appropriate ideas may never come to the fore and get adopted. To remedy this potential problem, along with choreographed *synergy*, I would suggest having choreographed *diversity* in your discussions and meetings. This requires seeking out individuals who have contrasting and nonconventional ideas and ways of viewing things. By doing this, you have the best chance to come up with the wisest range of effective ideas and strategies. Seek out those who think differently from you and your associates. Brilliance can come from the most unexpected places.

I believe it was Ben Grossman, the former editor of *Broadcasting & Cable* magazine, who, when discussing the subject of finding fresh ideas and new approaches for any company, said, "Try to find individuals from unconventional places to fill conventional positions."

Once again, choreographed diversity can bring a wellspring of new ideas to you and your company.

AUTHENTIC BELIEF IS ESSENTIAL FOR ALL CHOREOGRAPHERS

Optimism is the greatest gift that you can give yourself.
All things are possible when you believe!

—K.L.

Your belief in yourself and a success-evoking choreography are your fuel and your vehicles, respectively, for accomplishing greatness!

One thing that almost all individuals who attain consistent and sustained success have in common is their belief that they can achieve their *Goals*. Being armed with a success-evoking choreography and having attained success through achieving your mini-*Goals* and *Goals* should give you the valid belief and core confidence that you can and will live your *Dreams*.

THE AWESOME POWER OF FORGIVENESS

Forgiveness is a favor that you do for yourself.

—DR. HAROLD KUSHNER

You can be right and be miserable.

—RABBI DAVID WOZNICA

To err is human; to forgive is empowering.

—K.L.

Constructive choreographers understand that making mistakes in life is inevitable; the key is to forgive yourself and move on. Remember to forgive others as well and keep moving forward. As they say, "Grudges hurt the ones who hold them." However, as a wise choreographer, you may forgive, but you shouldn't forget, in the sense that you don't want to repeat the same mistake by detrimentally trusting or relying a second time on someone who doesn't deserve your trust or another opportunity to disappoint you. So forgive but be cautious thereafter.

CONTINUE TO EVOLVE

What punctures brilliance is a failure to evolve.

—COLIN COWHERD

My father often told me—and every day of his life, showed me—how essential it is for all choreographers to keep learning, growing, and evolving. This certainly was one of the main reasons why my dad was able to start a second major career at sixty-nine and thrive in his field until he was ninety-eight. Keep evolving and remain relevant and valuable.

CHOOSING TO EMULATE OR NOT EMULATE OTHERS

When I learned how to play paddle tennis, as a youngster, I did my best to emulate what top-tier players did—how they executed their strokes, how they acted, how they competed, and the like. This was one of the ways that I was able to quickly improve. As I matured, I transferred this strategy to every facet of my life. When I see someone who does something well or effectively, I try to incorporate it in some form or fashion into my behavioral repertoire.

On the other hand, I've also seen people act in highly inappropriate, self-defeating, and self-destructive ways, which I take note of and consciously work to never emulate.

I regard myself as a perpetual student of life, as I keep learning from people, experiences, and observations. My explicit *Goal* is to grow and evolve, and thereby become the very best person and professional I'm capable of being. This is a process that I recommend to my clients.

When starting out in the workforce or at any stage of your job, career, or professional development, take note and learn from everyone. See what talented and astute others do well, how they navigate challenging situations, and why people are or aren't successful. There are so many great teachers out there and valuable lessons to learn!

BE MINDFUL OF THE TIMES

There are no private moments. Everyone has a cell phone.

—PAT HADEN, director of USC athletics

I cannot count the number of career setbacks that individuals whom I know have suffered because they were photographed acting or otherwise appeared in a manner that was demeaning, embarrassing, and/or damaging to them or their employers.

Always remember that companies, employers, and college administrators believe that how you act or represent yourself is how you will act or represent *them*, and that there are no longer any "private moments." Be vigilant about protecting your reputation, image, and persona. One bad picture can damage you forever. So be mindful that we are living in a time in which "gotcha journalism" is everywhere.

In a similar vein, don't tweet or email anything that you could later regret. Before you press the send button, think things through as to how the content of what you write will be received by the recipients, and how it will affect, impact, and reflect upon *you* today and for years to come. Always be consequence cognizant!

THE POSITIVE BYPRODUCTS OF DOING THE RIGHT THING

[Having] integrity is doing the right thing when nobody's looking.
—COLIN COWHERD

There's no wrong time to do the right thing!
—MARK SCHLERETH, ESPN NFL expert
and former NFL player

*Act consistently with your ideal self, and great personal
and professional rewards will be yours.*

—K.L.

As a career coach to thousands of individuals, I have seen, learned, and counseled that if you do the right things and do things right, you develop high self-esteem, strong feelings of self-worth, and core confidence. These highly empowering feelings lead you to make more and more success-evoking career choices and steps, because you feel that you're worth doing good and great things for and that you and your career truly deserve the sweet fruits of success.

Conversely, if you make poor choices and act in a way that you're not proud of and know to be wrong, you develop low self-esteem, because you don't truly feel as if you have the goods to succeed or that you deserve good things in your life. A vicious cycle of poor, destructive choices and acts will, in all likelihood, follow.

So, as a success-evoking choreographer, do the right things and do things right . . . and soar!

FIND THE RIGHT POSITION FOR YOU WITH ANCILLARY HELP

Having the best and most appropriate resources on your side can contribute enormously to your successful job or position-attaining efforts. In fact, the right individuals can indeed be game-lifters and game-changers for you!

In your quest to find the right career and success-enhancing position, you may want to use ancillary resources such as head-hunters, employment agencies, agents, search firms, career-focused websites, social media, listings in newspapers (as well as other periodicals), and the like. Surely, an entire book can be written on the subject of ancillary job-attainment assistance; however, for Career Choreography purposes, let's touch on some core concepts, steps, and strategies regarding how to choose the right ancillary help for you, and how to secure a great job or position.

1. When using any kind of search resource, it is essential for those individuals representing you to understand who *you* are. This includes *your* values, *Goals*, and *Dreams*, as well as *your* strengths, non-strengths, and past experiences. If they are well acquainted with these elements—assuming these individuals are reputable, talented, engaged in the process, and well connected—then they are best positioned to accu-

rately articulate and demonstrate what makes you unique and highly qualified for a coveted position. The best means for you to ensure this type of informed representation is through a personal meeting—preferably out of the office in a quiet, relaxed setting. If a personal meeting cannot be arranged, a Zoom or Skype meeting, or the like, is your next best bet. If you can create a personal connection with the individuals who will assist in your job search, they will be far more likely to be invested in the process—which should increase your chances of success.

2. When using an individual or firm in your job-search process, it is important to employ the right one(s). Just as one talent agent isn't right for all potential clients and their particular needs, so, too, there will be job-search representatives and companies that may not be a good fit for you. Some firms specialize only in certain areas or types of positions; others have unique, high-level access within specific arenas or with high-profile individuals. In connection with this last point, if I were to need a particular or specialized form of heart or brain surgery, I would seek out the doctor who has the best track record for having done hundreds of successful surgeries like the one I'll need. You want an expert and specialist working with and for you, who has an excellent track record for securing a precise, career-enhancing result. Being an astute and success-evoking choreographer calls for you to do your homework and align yourself with the best and most effective teammate(s) for *you*.

3. Oftentimes, there is strength and efficiency in numbers. If you have the ability to work with a number of top-flight search firms or individuals simultaneously—and it is permissible to do so—you put the percentages of attaining success

in your favor by having as much broad-range access and saturation as possible.

4. In almost all instances, I recommend meeting a prospective employer in person, as you will have the opportunity to establish a positive connection and rapport, which can put you ahead of others who are being judged, at least initially, by a résumé alone. A number of my clients who took the initiative to secure a one-on-one, up-close-and-personal meeting with a potential employer—even if that employer didn't have the right position available at the time—wound up getting the job once one became available. In some instances, because a personal meeting went so well, the employer never considered conducting what might have been a time-consuming and costly job search; instead, the employer simply went right to our client and offered the coveted position.

I have found that "a particle in motion attracts other particles in motion." As a brilliant choreographer, be proactive and stay in motion by connecting with as many appropriate potential employers as possible. At the very least, you will hone your interviewing skills. In the best of all worlds, you will lay the foundation for being offered a wonderful opportunity in the future.

5. Knowledge is power, and it is often essential for securing the right position for you. So it is important to learn as much as you can about the availability of potential positions through job-search websites, social media, the Internet, seminars, newspapers and magazines, and so on. The more you know, the more exposure you have to potential employment opportunities, and the broader your reach and scope, the more

likely it is that you will secure enhancing job options from which to choose.

Career Choreography is all about strategically putting yourself in the best position to enjoy sustained career success. By taking advantage of all of the ancillary help available, you put yourself on a success-evoking path to secure a career-enhancing position.

＊＊＊＊＊＊

As we leave the choreography strategies portion of our journey, let's review the Four Principles of Career Choreography:

1. There is a logical, success-evoking choreography for accomplishing all professional *Goals*. The key is to construct and implement the most effective set of steps and strategies in order to attain your *Goals*.

2. Choreograph your Career by Consistently implementing Conscious, Constructive, success-evoking Choices made with Cognitive Clarity.

3. Every career decision you make and each career step you take should reflect your most important career values and bring you closer to attaining your career *Goals* and living your career *Dreams*.

4. Never make career decisions or act if your best judgment is clouded or dismantled by sabotaging emotions, impulses, or urges.

Part III

Attaining True Career and Life Happiness

THE IMPORTANCE OF PURSUING YOUR PASSION AND YOUR CALLING

If you love what you do,
you'll never work a day in your life.

—UNKNOWN

It is good to have an end to journey towards;
but it is the journey that matters in the end.

—PATTY TANNER,
sixth-grade schoolteacher extraordinaire

You can choose happiness!

—K.L.

Yⁿou will be much happier, and you will enjoy your work and
career a great deal more, if each day, you are pursuing your
calling—a job, career, or profession that your heart and gut tell

you that you were meant to do, or are inspired and highly motivated to do.

Individuals who are immersed in and passionate about what they do almost always fare far better than those who view their work as an obligation and nothing more than a means of earning a living or accumulating wealth. Those who pursue their calling—doing what they love while being challenged and stimulated—enjoy their work time and their careers so much more. They are also better in most instances at what they do than others, because they care about the quality of their work product. What a blessing for everyone involved!

As we discussed in the Heidi case study in Chapter 4, not only was Heidi a successful art-gallery owner, but more important, she loved being immersed in the art world, discovering and providing support to new artists, and doing charity work in connection with her gallery.

By identifying the things she did well, along with those that made her heart sing, Heidi designed a personal path that led her to enjoy sustained happiness, fulfillment, and life-meaning.

If I won the lottery, I wouldn't change a thing professionally. What I do truly makes my heart sing! When I wake up in the morning, I can't wait to get started. Why? Because the acts I perform each day bring me joy, satisfaction, and feelings of self-worth, and because I'm being of service to others.

Our daughter, Mary, and our son, Tristan, are twins and are starting their freshman year of college. Fortunately, both Tristan and Mary appear to have found their academic and professional callings. What a wonderful blessing for them and for us as their parents, as we see their joy, excitement, and clear sense of direction as they plan their college courses, with Tristan wanting to become an architect and Mary wanting to work with special-needs children.

When we were in the car together recently, I asked Tristan how he knows that architecture is his calling. He quickly responded, "When the inspiration hits me, there's nothing like it!" When I asked him to tell me more, he explained that he loves visualizing a design and then figuring out how to make his vision a reality. He went on to say that the feeling of completing a project is "incredible!"

I have witnessed him spend endless extra hours to work on and complete his high-school architecture projects. Why? Because he loved what he was doing. It's his calling!

In Mary's case, she, like her mom, has an amazing voice and adores singing. She also loves interacting with children and being a radiant light in their lives. Until last summer, we thought Mary was going to pursue singing. But when she worked as a teaching assistant at the Down Syndrome Foundation of Orange County, she had what she calls a "major epiphany," which was that working with special-needs children truly makes her heart sing and is her calling. In light of this, Mary shared an essay she had written for an education class. Here are the last few beautiful sentences:

> Now armed with the knowledge of what my gifts are, and the confidence to utilize them to make a positive impact, I can carry on and not be afraid of altering my plans as my life unfolds. I am not afraid of the epiphanies or the dead ends. I am aware that they are part of my process of discovering a career, a vocation, and most importantly, my calling. I now always tell people who have earned my trust that Special Education is one of the purest manifestations of God's love that there is. I tell them this because I feel it in my heart and I truly know that the Special Ed classroom is where God wants me to be.

My wonderfully talented wife, Melinda, was one of ten siblings lovingly raised by Mary and Ross Myers. With her extraordinary mom as her role model, Melinda always knew that her calling was to have children and be the most attentive and loving mom possible. But along with her parental calling, Melinda is blessed to have a beautiful voice—so good, in fact, that she sang title songs for theatrical films before having children. So singing was Melinda's other calling. Once she gave birth to Mary and Tristan, however, she gladly stopped singing professionally to pursue her main calling, which was raising our children. Now that Mary and Tristan are starting college, I see and feel Melinda's passion and excitement welling up because she is singing again. She and her soul are lit up!

Identifying and pursuing your calling is absolutely a major positive life game-changer, as well as a huge boon to your mental and physical health. Life can be short—enjoy it and make the very most of it by doing the things you love!

48

YOU DON'T NEED
TO BE THE RICHEST
ONE IN THE CEMETERY

While happiness can come along with success, success isn't a guarantee that you will be happy, personally or professionally. In fact, some of the most successful individuals I've known are miserable. Just look at all the celebrities and pro athletes who appear to have attained incredible success, yet time after time, they commit self-destructive acts.

I'll never forget the story that my dad told me, when I was young, about the alluring opportunity he was given to begin his own department-store chain. At the time, my dad was the executive vice president of his firm. He was renowned in his business as an excellent merchandiser, master negotiator, and unparalleled teacher. He did well financially, but we were by no means wealthy. Because my dad had no formal education (as he would say, he went to the school of hard knocks), he always felt the need to work oppressively long hours (six days and some evenings each week). As a result, my mom and I spent very little time with him during my growth years.

Finally, when my dad no longer had to work weekends and only had to work one night a week, he was offered a lucrative opportunity to strike out on his own—with substantial financial backing—to start a new chain of off-price department stores. If he had accepted the offer, his salary would have increased substantially. If things went well, his income would have grown exponentially. He also, once again, would have had to work grueling hours.

But for the first time in my dad's life, he had achieved *balance*. He and I spent wonderful weekends together. He and my mom played tennis and went to the movies regularly. Because of this, their love and camaraderie grew by leaps and bounds. With my dad's new schedule, we had dinners together many times a week, whereas we had rarely spent dinnertime together before. And he loved his job!

The day my dad turned down the offer to start his own chain of stores in order to keep his current, fulfilling life intact, he explained, "Kenny, I never want to be the richest guy in the cemetery. I see people get burned out and shriveled up because they have an ego that pushes them to keep conquering, keep competing, keep staying in the limelight—when it's not necessary. They are so caught up in all the bullshit that they forget what's really important. The ones you love, your health, true happiness—*they're* important! I love you. I love Betty. I have my health. I love what I do and where we live.

"People risk their families and their health for fame and fortune. Why would I want to risk losing all I have—all that we have? Who needs their offer or their money? We've always had enough. We've never wanted for anything. Kenny, I've never been jealous or envious of anyone. Jealousy consumes people and eats them up.

"My father died when I was four. I loved him very much, but I never got to really know my dad. Life can be short. Don't let it pass you by.

"When I came over [from Poland], I had to help support our family, so I had to begin working immediately. I had no schooling. I couldn't speak English. No one thought that I had any ability or future. I had to work like a dog to get where I am. I had to keep proving myself over and over again. But I don't need to prove anything to anyone anymore! I'm one lucky son-of-a-gun. I have so many blessings in my life, and I know it! I'm turning down the offer."

For the first time in my dad's life, he had attained the blessing of professional inner peace and life-work balance; he was truly happy, both personally and professionally. He may well have been a "lucky son-of-a-gun" to have all of these gifts in his life at the same time. But just as important, he was a *wise* "son-of-a-gun" in both appreciating his good fortune and taking the appropriate, constructive steps to preserve his blessings.

My dad has been and continues to be a great role model and teacher for me, because of the insights he's shared with me and the examples he has set. One of the foremost things about him that always sticks in my mind is that he loved and cherished nearly every minute of his career, from the day he started out as a seventeen-year-old boy in the receiving room until the day he retired.

How many people can honestly say that? Very few.

Growing up, I always marveled at how my dad couldn't wait—literally—to go to work each morning. He loved talking about work-related issues with my mom and his colleagues. His work challenged, excited, and invigorated him. It kept him sharp and vital and gave him a sense of being valued and relevant. The reason he was able to derive all of these benefits is because every day, he did something that made his heart sing! His work was a true passion. It was in every way his calling.

Unlike some, who go to work and watch the clock and their lives tick away, who are unhappy or bored with what they do at their workplace, or who feel trapped in their tragically unfulfilling careers because of expectations and responsibilities that have been put upon them, or they foolishly put on themselves, my dad fully enjoyed his two separate careers that spanned over eighty years! He would be the first to tell you that it was his work that in large part kept him so healthy—in mind, body, and spirit. And it kept him healthy enough to work until he was ninety-eight.

Before my dad passed away, he took my hand and said, "Kenny, I truly have no regrets. I have you and Betty, so I have *everything* I could *ever* want. And look what I accomplished. I'm so lucky!"

When my dad was buried a few days later, one thing was crystal clear: Although he never aspired to it, he truly was the richest guy in the cemetery!

The point here is that you can consciously *choose*—if you value your physical and emotional well-being—to pursue a job, profession, or career that makes your heart sing. And if you do, you will be putting the percentages heavily in your favor that you will love what you do. You will be excited, challenged, and fulfilled by what you do. You will make the most of your precious life, and you will put yourself in a wonderful position to preserve and enhance your emotional and physical well-being. These are blessings that you can choose to put into your life, and those who love you and want the best for you will want you to enjoy them.

Finally, if you do things not only to enhance yourself but also to enhance others, you will feel great about what you're doing with your life, and you will also give your life great meaning. This will raise your feelings of self-esteem and self-worth, as well as your self-image. All of these good feelings will lead you to develop empowering feelings of self-love—which will motivate you to do more good things for yourself, because you'll feel that you are worth doing good things for.

These are all wonderful reasons to create a profession for yourself that makes your heart sing and allows other singing hearts to harmonize with yours!

Remember, at the end of the day, and at the end of your life, it doesn't matter whether or not you'll be the richest or most famous guy or gal in the cemetery. As the Greeks essentially wrote, "It doesn't matter how you die, but whether you *truly lived.*"

Are you truly living? Is your heart singing? If not, start choreographing!

For now, this is the end of our time together. However, it is the beautiful beginning of the rest of your life as a great choreographer.

One last thought.

Success in life doesn't necessarily bring happiness, but if you're truly happy with yourself and with your life, you are a huge success!

I wish you the very best.

AUTHOR'S NOTE

A few weeks after my dad's passing, Ben Cammarata, the chairman of the TJX Companies, my dad's one-time buyer trainee, and eventually his T.J. Maxx employer, sent my mom and me this letter.

May 10, 2007

Dear Betty and Kenny,

As saddened as I am by Jack's passing, I can't begin to tell you how privileged I was to share his 100th birthday with him and both of you. I'll never forget the smile on his face and twinkle in his eyes.

As you know, Jack and I knew each other for 45 years. He was my mentor and my dear friend. I learned something new and different about the business each time I spoke to him. His knowledge about off-price retailing is unsurpassed in our industry.

Jack will always be the "King of Negotiation" and a true pioneer in the development of new frontiers in sportswear manufacturing, including Hong Kong, Paris, Milan, Los Angeles, Miami and more.

Jack lived his life loving his Betty and Kenny. Also, he lived the retail business more than anyone I've ever known. Jack Lindner was bigger than life and a true legend in our business.

I will miss Jack terribly and will always be grateful for the opportunity he gave me and his major contributions to the TJX Companies.

Love,
Ben Cammarata

ACKNOWLEDGMENTS

I would like to acknowledge the wonderful support I always receive from my loving family and our adorable doggies, Clara, Bert, and Peanut, as well as from our guinea pig, Weegee. You all make my heart and soul sing, and each and every day you light up my life. I so love you all, forever and always!

I acknowledge my incredible parents, Betty and Jack. You have always loved me unconditionally and completely, and have been there for me, happily sacrificed for me, and given me the rock-solid, emotional foundation to enable and empower me to live many of my *Dreams*. From you, Mom, I have developed a deep love of psychology and the study of people; from you, Dad, as reflected in this book, I have learned much of what I know about business and choreographing careers. Thank you both so much; I love you endlessly and always.

I acknowledge the love and support of my extended family: my grandparents, uncles, aunts, cousins, nieces, nephews, the Berman family, the Myers family, the Havens family, the Cammarata family, the Hartley family, our fantastic and loyal Ken Lindner & Associates, Inc., clients who have entrusted us with choreographing their precious careers and from whom I've learned so much, and to my KLA family, who have always been there with and for me.

I acknowledge the support and love of all of my dear friends. I so treasure and appreciate you all.

I thank the individuals who were kind enough to take their valuable time to write a book endorsement.

I acknowledge some special individuals, without whose help and support this book would never have been written: my terrific executive assistant, Shari Freis (only the most superlative adjectives can describe Shari!); my wonderful, sage counselor and long-time friend, Marty Singer; my stellar typist and advisor, Edward Miller; Mel Berger (whom I cannot appreciate and respect more); and the wonderful individuals at Greenleaf Publishing who are amazing in every way, and have always seen the best in me and my work.

Finally, I thank you, the reader. I sincerely hope that you have substantially benefited from reading this book. I wish you the very best in all of your future endeavors.

Career Choreography is a heartfelt thank-you to you all.

APPENDIX

1. YOUR *GOAL LIST*

Your *Goal List* comprises what you would like to do professionally and/or what you would like to accomplish in your job, position, profession, and/or your career. These are your aspirations. For example—

1. "I'd like to be a speech therapist."

2. "I'd love to run an art gallery."

3. "I'd like to work in some capacity for a magazine."

4. "I'd like to be a court stenographer."

5. "I'd love to make my college basketball team."

6. "I'd like to be a trial lawyer."

7. "I'd love to be an actor/actress."

8. "I'd like to work in the car manufacturing business."

9. "I'd love to be a physical therapist."

10. "I'd like to advance in my company."

11. "I'd love to be a makeup artist."

12. "I'd like to work at a fast-food restaurant and one day own one."

13. "I'd love to be a novelist."

14. "I'd love to be a sports agent."

On the following page, please list all of the job- and career-related *Goals* that you would like to achieve. Take your time and search deep down for your responses. Also, keep in mind that these are *your Goals* exclusively, not your significant other's, parents', siblings', teachers', or advisors' expectations for you.

YOUR *GOAL LIST*

1. _____
   _____

2. _____
   _____

3. _____
   _____

4. _____
   _____

5. _____
   _____

6. _____
   _____

7. _____
   _____

8. _____
   _____

9. _____

10. _____

11. _____

12. _____

13. _____

2. YOUR *DREAM LIST*

Your *Dream List* comprises your professional *Dreams*. Your *Dream(s)* is/are what you want most, professionally. They are what all of the steps you've carefully crafted lead to. They are your ultimate destination! For example—

1. "I'd love to own a McDonald's (or a chain of them)."

2. "I'd love to play professional tennis."

3. "I'd love to own a hair salon."

4. "I'd love to be a partner in my accounting firm."

5. "I'd love to be a speech therapist."

6. "I'd love to be a successful real estate broker."

7. "I'd love to play in a band and perform at cool venues."

8. "I'd love to be Miss America."

9. "I'd love to be a news anchor in my hometown."

10. "I'd love to own my own vacation resort."

11. "I'd love to be an educator at my old high school."

12. "I'd love to have an important position at the steel plant I work at."

13. "I'd love to be a merchandise manager for my department-store chain."

Once again, on the following page, please list your *Dream(s)*. These are the professional aspirations that truly would make your heart sing! And please keep in mind that these are *your Dreams*—not the *Dreams* or expectations of others that have been foisted upon you.

YOUR *DREAM LIST*

1. _____
   _____

2. _____
   _____

3. _____
   _____

4. _____
   _____

5. _____
   _____

6. _____
   _____

7. _____
   _____

3. YOUR *CLARIFYING LIST* #1

WHAT DO YOU LOVE/LIKE TO DO?

Before working on this *List*, please review my *Clarifying List* on pages 31 and 32, as well as those of Heidi and Sarah in Chapter 4. These are excellent examples of how to make your *List*.

Now, take all the time you need to search your heart, mind, and soul to identify what you truly enjoy doing or would love/like to do in your job, profession, and/or career. This way, you will clearly recognize some of the things and qualities that you require for or want to incorporate into your professional life.

Once you have done this, please make your *List*.

1. _____
   _____

2. _____
   _____

3. _____
   _____

4. _____

_____

5. _____

_____

6. _____

_____

7. _____

_____

8. _____

_____

9. _____

_____

10. _____

_____

11. _____

_____

12. _____

_____

13. _____

_____

4. YOUR *CLARIFYING LIST #2*

WHAT DON'T YOU LIKE DOING?

As you did above, please review my *Clarifying List* on pages 32 and 33. Then, once again, dig deep and identify what you *don't* want to do and *don't* want in your professional life. By doing this, you will clearly know what you want to avoid in your job, position, and career.

Once you have taken the time to do this, please make your *List*.

1. _____

2. _____

3. _____

4. _____

5. _____

6. _____

7. _____

8. _____

9. _____

_____

10. _____

_____

11. _____

_____

12. _____

_____

13. _____

_____

5. YOUR REVIEW PROCESS

Once you have completed your two *Clarifying Lists*, put them aside for a few days, and then with fresh eyes review your responses to see if they truly reflect how you feel and what you want. If additions or modifications need to be made, please make them now.

After doing this, please review your responses and put a star after the ones that are your most important and compelling. For example, on my *Clarifying List* #1, I would star that whatever job or position I take *must* incorporate dealing with and having lots of interactions with people. Why? Because I love being with and learning from people, as well as being a bright, encouraging light in their lives. Additionally, I have strong people skills and people trust me.

I would also star my love of marketing. I love marketing and figuring out compelling reasons why you should buy what I'm selling. Of course, I only represent the people and concepts I truly believe in, so the individuals with whom I interact feel my authentic passion for my client or the project that I'm marketing.

Additionally, I would star the fact that I love being an entrepreneur— designing my own path and strategies, and determining my own fate. Being an only child, playing singles in tennis, and having to get used to navigating things on my own certainly contributed to my highly valuing these abilities.

Okay, now it's your turn to star the things that are essential for you to enjoy in your job, position, and career. Or, put another way, these are your professional "must haves"! Please begin when you're ready.

Upon completing the *Clarifying List* #1 starring process, please go to your *Clarifying List* #2, and star the things that you *do not* want and those you need to avoid in your job, position, and career. For example, as I discuss in Chapter 4, once I worked for a corporate law firm, I realized that I *do not* want a job where I deal mostly with documents and projects; I do not want to work in a noncreative, conformist, fear-driven work environment; and I *do not* want to work for individuals who don't view me and my talents as special and/or don't highly value me, as I know that I am exponentially more effective when I work with and for individuals who believe in me.

Now it's your turn to star the things that you *do not* want in your professional life.

Once you have starred your essential *wants* and *don't wants*, please look them over carefully, as this review will clarify what kinds of jobs, positions, and professions are the most appropriate, satisfying, and heart- and soul-nourishing for you, as they tap into and make the most of your professional preferences and passions.

6. YOUR *SHORE UP LIST*

Now, please compile your *Shore Up List* so that you clearly identify, recognize, and keep at top of mind what professional and educational experiences you need in order to develop your strongest professional foundation. By doing this, you put yourself in the very best position to secure the right job or profession for you, and once you secure it, you enjoy sustained success and fulfillment.

As you have done earlier with your *Clarifying Lists*, please think carefully and honestly about what professional and educational experiences you need to shore up your skill-set foundation and résumé, so that you put the percentages strongly in your favor that you will secure the job or position you covet and then shine in it.

Once you're ready to fill out your *List*, please do so below.

1. _____
   _____

2. _____
   _____

3. _____
   _____

4. _____
   _____

5. _____
   _____

6. _____
   _____

7. _____

_____

8. _____

_____

9. _____

_____

10. _____

_____

When you have completed this *List*, with great gusto, start figuring out how to have these essential experiences and thereby make yourself the most attractive job candidate and professional you're capable of being.

7. YOUR *CHOREOGRAPHY LIST*

When filling out your *Choreography List*, there are some helpful steps that you can take.

1. At the top of your *List*, write down your *Goal* or *Dream*. This *Goal* or *Dream* is what all of the steps that you take are meant to lead up to and help you to achieve.

2. At the bottom of your *List*, please write where you are starting from today. For example: I am out of work and want to find a job that makes the most of my skills; I'm just finishing college/grad school; I'm working, but I need to make a beneficial change of jobs or professions, as I'm not happy (enough); I've been out of work for many years to raise my child/children and I now want to find a job that's fulfilling.

3. Your next step is to seek out credible advice from those who should know and from those you trust, as to what they perceive accomplishing your career *Goals* and living your career *Dreams* will or might entail. The more homework you can do, the more you can learn, and the fewer false starts you make, the better.

4. Looking at what you aspire to accomplish (#1 above) and where you're starting from (#2 above), ask yourself and write down, line by line, what professional and educational experiences you need to give you the qualifications and the very best chance to land the job or position you want.

5. For example, do you need to take courses or get a degree in a certain area to lay the best foundation for success? And/or do you need to get certain on-the-job experiences to shore up your skill set and résumé? If the answer is yes, please add it/them to your *List*.

6. As you get going on your choreography journey and are immersed in the process, continue to ask questions, observe others in your chosen field, and learn as much as you can from every experience and everyone. This should give you excellent insights as to what your best future choreography steps need to be.

7. Your next step is to creatively use everything you learn to put the percentages squarely in your favor that you will achieve your *Goals* and live your *Dreams*. For example, figure out who your allies are, who believes in you, who benefits from your career growth, who your detractors are, and so on. At the end of the day, it will be a certain few individuals who have the power to advance your career or stall it; make sure you know who has that power, and who's on your side. Also,

make sure that the individuals in the decision-making positions and your allies know everything good that you're doing and accomplishing for them.

8. As you continue to learn, grow, and evolve, keep modifying your choreography so that you are taking the wisest and most effective steps toward achieving your professional *Goals* and living your *Dreams*.

As we discuss throughout *Career Choreography*, even the most adept choreographers take missteps. When this happens, don't let it get you down; it's part of the process. Just learn from the experience and figure out a better and more beneficial next step and take it. Put your mistakes in your rear-view mirror, and with great optimism and focus drive forward!

From time to time your choreography may have to be modified or completely abandoned if your values, *Goals*, and/or *Dreams* change. So please keep monitoring any changes in your aspirations and values. Also, as you accumulate more knowledge and have additional experiences, your choreography steps may need tweaking. Remember, this is a positive part of your choreography process.

Once you're ready to fill out your *Choreography List*, please do so below.

Here's to you securing fantastic results!

1. _____
   _____

2. _____
   _____

3. _____

   _____

4. _____

   _____

5. _____

   _____

6. _____

   _____

7. _____

   _____

8. _____

   _____

9. _____

   _____

10. _____

    _____

11. _____

    _____

12. _____

    _____

13. _____

    _____

ABOUT THE AUTHOR

KEN LINDNER is the founder of Positive Life Choice Psychology™ and the Positive Life Choice Psychology Lifestyle™. Ken's calling is to envision what can be in people and to craft the steps that turn their great potential into a highly positive and productive reality. He graduated from Harvard University, magna cum laude; from Cornell Law School; from Brooklyn Polytechnic Preparatory Country Day School (Brooklyn Poly Prep); and from the Brooklyn Ethical Culture School.

In addition to *Career Choreography*™, Ken is the author of four books: *Your Killer Emotions: The 7 Steps to Mastering the Toxic Emotions, Urges, and Impulses That Sabotage You*, in which he shares with readers how to master their emotions and break their destructive behavioral patterns and bad habits; *Crunch Time! 8 Steps to Making the Right Life Decisions at the Right Times*, which gives readers the tried-and-true emotionally intelligent life strategies that will enable them to fulfill their greatest potentials; and Editions 1 and 2 of *Broadcasting Realities*, which equip broadcast journalists and aspiring broadcast journalists with the essential information they need to make constructive career decisions. At the heart of all of these books is the concept that your life choices are precious, and if made wisely and strategically, they can change your life in the most beneficial and wonderful ways.

Ken is married to his wife, Melinda, and they are blessed to have twins, Mary and Tristan. They also have three adorable dogs, Peanut, Bert, and Clara. The Lindners live in Los Angeles, California.